1-2

√
4 00
B-128

# RUBENS

*and his world*

# RUBENS
*and his world*

BY CHRISTOPHER WHITE

A STUDIO BOOK

THE VIKING PRESS · NEW YORK

*To M.L.*

*Published in 1968 by The Viking Press, Inc.*
*625 Madison Avenue, New York, N.Y.10022*

*Printed in Great Britain by Jarrold and Sons Ltd, Norwich*

ANTWERPEN.

Die Schelde.

A view of Antwerp from the River Scheldt with the spire of the Cathedral in the centre

THE LIFE OF Peter Paul Rubens appears to us as much a work of art as any of those that came from his brush. Every action or meeting seemed a preordained step leading logically towards the next important occasion. His life developed in sonata form, culminating in a coda of glorious warmth. But the opening phrases were sombre. Political storms and personal misfortunes heralded the birth of Peter Paul Rubens in 1577. His father, Jan Rubens, whose family history in Antwerp can be traced back to the end of the fourteenth century, had no sooner become a successful advocate and alderman of his home town and married a certain Maria Pypelinx, than war broke out in the name of religion, but in the cause of politics.

It is often only in adversity that depth of character is revealed, and in no instance could this have been truer than Rubens' parents. Had political misfortunes not overtaken Jan Rubens, we should probably remember him today as a worthy citizen of Antwerp, as a successful advocate and a serious alderman, as a solid respectable citizen who had the honour of being the father of one of the world's greatest artists. He would have been considered a man of parts. The painter's mother, on the other hand, would probably have been no more than a name, and we would have granted her respectability. But fate decreed otherwise, and for the benefit of posterity a merciless spotlight was trained on the different characters of Rubens' parents, revealing the strength of one and the weakness of the other. The blood that ran in their son's veins was mixed with extremes of sterling fortitude and easygoing intelligence. His ultimate strength of character could not have been taken for granted, and possibly his genius was sparked by the very different characteristics he inherited from each parent.

5

The submerged momentum of the Reformation in the Low Countries burst forth with the death of Charles V, who had been a powerful though respected ruler. He was succeeded by his son Philip, whose strong leanings towards Spain and Catholicism rapidly offended the Flemish nobles. The latter espoused the cause of the Reformation largely for political purposes, and Protestantism spread rapidly throughout the Low Countries, leading to widespread iconoclasm by 1566. Philip swiftly retaliated, and the Duke of Alva, with no less ardour and bestiality than his spiritual heirs of four centuries later, carried out a relentless persecution in Flanders. In the spirit of the times, Jan Rubens had previously become a Calvinist in practice. Now, after a little specious pleading of his Catholic orthodoxy to the Spanish suppressors, he had the wit to see that his home country was no longer a safe place to live, and in 1568 he fled to Cologne with his wife and four children. But there his religious beliefs caused further trouble, and under the threat of expulsion he gave positive proof of his orthodoxy. He had made his gesture of religious independence and that was sufficient for him.

If the weakness of his religious convictions led to convenient results, his sexual indiscretions were not so easily glossed over. In 1568 he became the legal adviser and confidant of Anne of Saxony, Princess of Orange, who had been left behind in Cologne by her husband, William of Orange, while he raised reinforcements in Germany for his battle against the Spanish. In this situation, the weak character of Jan Rubens was no match for the sensuality of the ugly, pleasure-loving princess. By the spring of the following year the true nature of their relationship was

Antwerp town hall in flames. Detail of a painting by an Antwerp Master of the sixteenth century

The Castle of Dillenburg where Jan Rubens was imprisoned, from a drawing by
Frans Post

sufficiently obvious for all to see, and the elder Rubens was arrested and imprisoned on a charge of adultery. The child conceived during the course of
intimate evenings spent in the small town of Siegen, where Anne had moved
from Cologne, was born in August.

In Germany the penalty for adultery was death, and, imprisoned in the
dungeons of the Castle of Dillenburg, Jan Rubens gave way to despair. It was at
this moment that his wife became a character in her own right and took the
centre of the stage. Having recovered from the news of her husband's betrayal,
she took up her pen to plead on his behalf, addressing a heartfelt petition 'written
without art or learning' to the prince and princess. To her husband, Maria
Pypelinx wrote a letter of forgiveness, but she had hardly finished it, when she
received one, in a very different vein, from him. She immediately sent a reply,
'written this first of April between midnight and one o'clock,' which reveals her
nobility of character, forgiveness and fortitude in the face of adversity. 'Dear and
beloved husband, after I had written you the enclosed letter, the messenger we
had sent to you arrived bringing me a letter from you, which gave me joy because
I see from it that you are satisfied with my forgiveness. I never thought you would
have believed that there would be any difficulty about that from me, for in
truth I made none. How could I have the heart to be angry with you in such peril,
when were it possible I would give my life to save you . . . . Be assured then that
I have forgiven you completely. Please God that may suffice to set you free. We
should soon have cause to rejoice; but I find nothing in your letter to console me,

*Imprisonment
of father*

7

for it has broken my heart by showing me you have lost courage and speak as if you were on the point of death. I am so troubled that I know not what I am writing. One would think that I desired your death since you ask me to accept it in expiation. Alas, how you hurt me by saying that. In truth it passes my endurance. If there is no more pity where shall I find a refuge? Where must I seek it? I will ask it of Heaven with tears and cries.' And she added at the end, 'Say no more "your unworthy husband" for all is forgiven.'

*Move to Cologne*    After two years of pleading with the House of Nassau, Maria Pypelinx finally secured her husband's release on bail. But the strictest conditions were attached, including permanent residence in Siegen, where they lived half-imprisoned but happily reunited, and only in 1578 was Jan Rubens finally pardoned and allowed to live anywhere he wanted, except territory belonging to the House of Nassau and the Low Countries. The family lost no time in shaking off the dust of Siegen and returned to Cologne. During their time together in Siegen, their reconciliation had been celebrated with the birth of two sons, Philip, in 1573, and Peter Paul, in 1577. When they departed from Siegen the drama was nearly over, but the scars remained. Just how much it meant to the two sons, only infants when they left for Cologne, is made clear by their avoidance of acknowledging Siegen as the place of their birth. The small town could have been no more than a name to them, but they did their best to eliminate it from their family history. Indeed, its hidden influence on Peter Paul probably did not stop there, and may well have given an extra fillip to his ambition.

Life in Cologne cannot have been easy, though straitened circumstances were probably softened by the happiness of family life. In later years Peter Paul Rubens was to recall, 'I have great affection for the city of Cologne, because it was there

A view of Siegen in the sixteenth century

8

*Silenus surprised by the water nymph Aegle*, detail from a drawing made shortly after Rubens' return from Italy

that I was brought up until the tenth year of my life.' Their income had been sacrificed to rescue Jan Rubens, and to make matters worse, he was once again ordered to go to Siegen to await the prince's disposition. After further entreaties from his wife, and further payments from the family fortune, Jan Rubens was pardoned absolutely, and was able to take up his profession again, establishing himself in the esteem of Prince Charles de Croy. He only had, however, a few years of life left, and in 1587 he died in Cologne. In Siegen the family had belonged to the Lutheran Church, but on their return to Cologne they returned to the Catholic faith, which became the religion of their children.

The widow soon went back with her three surviving children to her home *Return to Antwerp* town of Antwerp, from which she had fled some twenty years before. Her financial situation must have greatly improved by this time, since she went to live in a house in the Meir, the largest square in the city. Peter Paul continued his studies in a school run by a certain Rombout Verdonck, situated in the cemetery behind the choir of Notre-Dame. There he met a boy, three years younger than

9

himself, Balthasar Moretus, who was destined to be a lifelong friend, and to achieve eminence as head of the famous Plantin printing house. A few years later Moretus wrote to Rubens' brother Philip that 'he knew his brother at school and *amavi lectissimi ac suavissimi ingenii juvenem*'. At school the boys learned Latin and some Greek. On the syllabus were such books as Plutarch's *Education of Children*, Cicero, and the *Aeneid* and *Bucolics* of Virgil. The last-named work inspired a drawing of some years later, which shows the water nymph Aegle rubbing Silenus' brow with blood-red mulberries; the god has been bound hand and foot in order to make him carry out his promise to sing a song, which he now laughingly does. Nearer in time to his schooldays were the copies he made from illustrated books, particularly those with woodcuts by Tobias Stimmer, which Rubens recalled many years later when he travelled on a barge from Utrecht to Amsterdam with Sandrart. His artistic imagination was stirred at an early age by what he saw and read.

Rubens did not remain in Verdonck's school for long, and at the age of thirteen his academic training was virtually over. During the course of his years of schooling, however, he absorbed a great deal. His familiarity with Latin was wide enough for him not only to draw on the literature for subject-matter without a moment's hesitation, but also, in spite of his constant protestations to the contrary, to write it fluently. His letters were full of Latin quotations and allusions, and he was never at a loss for an apt phrase. Latin was not his only language, and, as his letters show, he wrote fluently in French, Italian and Spanish. Whether he learned them at school or later on his travels, he certainly picked up a sufficient knowledge to correspond freely in the various tongues, and only rarely did he write in Flemish, which was then, as it generally is now, considered a vulgar tongue to be reserved for speech.

*Service at the Lalaing court*

When Rubens left school, according to his nephew, 'he was soon placed by his mother in the service of the noble lady Marguerite de Ligne, widow of Philip, Count of Lalaing, where he remained some time as her page.' She was probably living at Audenarde at the time the young Rubens joined her court. His mother presumably had aspirations to make her son into a courtier, but he, a person with ideas of his own, quickly tired of the small enclosed circle, with its unsympathetic daily routine and strict etiquette. The leisurely atmosphere of a widow's court can hardly have been stimulating to a young and active man. By itself it was not a very important moment in the artist's life, but it gave him his first familiarity with court life, which was to play such an important part throughout his career, even though he took every opportunity to escape from it. His reactions to life at Audenarde foretold his future feelings about all the major courts of Europe.

The reasons that drove Rubens to ask his mother to remove him were possibly as much due to his growing desire to paint as to his dislike of life at Audenarde. He had already tried his hand with a pen in a number of drawings of medieval tombs belonging to the Lalaing family, which though a little thick and rigid have his unmistakable personality about them. And it is significant that his first

Two drawings made by Rubens after
woodcuts by Tobias Stimmer

Costume studies probably made from
tombs of members of the Lalaing and
other families, now part of Rubens'
*Costume Book*

The painter Adam van Noort, the second of Rubens' masters, from the etching by Van Dyck (detail)

known works are copies after other works of art of an earlier century. For the whole of his life he retained a reverence for and a passionate interest in the art of the past, which was not only reflected in his own works, but can be seen in the copies he continued to make. There could be no better place for a young man to nurse a feeling for the past than the Lalaing circle, even if he quickly outgrew its narrow limitations.

*Artistic training*    The urge to paint was all-powerful. He returned to his mother's house in Antwerp and was apprenticed to a landscape artist, Tobias Verhaecht, who was related to him. He can only have spent a short time with him before he moved on to the studio of another Antwerp artist, Adam van Noort. Though no trace of this master's influence can be seen in Rubens' earliest surviving works, he apparently stayed four years there before changing studios once again, this time putting himself under the tutelage of Otto van Veen. Towards the end of his stay in van Veen's studio he would have witnessed the preparation of the decorations carried out for the triumphal entry of Archduke Albert and his wife Isabella in 1599, and may even have taken part in this project. If so, it represents his first contact with two patrons who were to play a very important part in his life.

The copy made by Rubens
in Venice after Titian's
painting *Abraham and Isaac*,
at that time in the Church
of Santo Spirito

Rubens undoubtedly learned the rudiments of art in his home country, but *Visit to Italy* artistic education of a higher order began with his arrival in Italy in 1600. During the eight years he spent there, both his character and his art matured. From a formal and correct figure, he developed into a man of the world and a confident painter. According to his nephew, he went straight to Venice. Even if the young artist has unfortunately left us no written record of his impressions of the city and its inhabitants, his painting speaks eloquently of his deep admiration for Venetian art, and his stay in the city provided him with his first opportunity to savour its delights in any quantity. Possibly at this stage of his visit his thoughts were more occupied with finding a position that would give him protection and financial support. Chance played into his hands when he found himself staying in the same lodging as a gentleman in the service of Vincenzo de Gonzaga, Duke of

Mantua, to whom he showed his pictures, and who in turn put them before the duke when he came on a visit to Venice in July. Gonzaga, who had a collector's mania, not only for works of art but also for artists, was sufficiently impressed to take Rubens into his service. He already had one Fleming attached to his court, and only a month after Rubens' appointment he was to add yet another, Frans Pourbus the Younger. Rubens promptly joined the duke's retinue and was immediately taken off to the handsome, grim city of Mantua, surrounded by swamps and flat land reminiscent of his native country. But if Mantua lacked the romantic character of Venice, it had much to offer in compensation.

*The House of Gonzaga*

Mantua was one of the capitals of the dozen or so small states that made up northern Italy at the time, and like its neighbouring rulers, such as the Este in Ferrara and the Farnese in Parma, the House of Gonzaga had a long tradition in the patronage of the fine arts. In the fifteenth century Mantegna had decorated one of the rooms of the medieval ducal palace with frescoes in honour of the Gonzaga family, and in the following century Giulio Romano had added to the ducal residences by designing and largely decorating the Palazzo del Tè. As well as commissioning permanent adornments to the city, the Gonzaga family – Vincenzo no less than the others – avidly collected paintings and owned works by artists such as Raphael, Titian and Correggio. Poetry, theatre and music also flourished under the patronage of Gonzaga, and during his stay Rubens must have been intimately acquainted with the duke's master of music, Claudio Monteverdi, who, during three years, was occupied with composing his opera *Orfeo*. Vincenzo was by no means an aesthete whose pleasures were confined to the fine arts, but followed in the Renaissance-princely tradition of collecting all kinds of exotica, as well as enjoying full-bloodedly the more sensual earthly pleasures. Mantua must have been a refreshing change from the austere court of the widowed Countess of Lalaing, and many years later, when the city fell to the Imperial troops, Rubens nostalgically recalled how he had 'Served the House of Gonzaga for many years, and enjoyed a delightful residence in that country in my youth.'

A bird's-eye view of Mantua

The Camera degli Sposi in the Palazzo Ducale, Mantua, decorated with frescoes by
Andrea Mantegna

The garden front of the Palazzo del Tè, Mantua, built by Giulio Romano

Gonzaga had the restlessness that goes with such wide tastes and was constantly travelling. Rubens had no sooner settled in his new occupation than he was taken in his master's retinue to Florence to witness the proxy marriage between his sister-in-law Marie de Médicis and Henry IV of France. The event was celebrated in truly sumptuous style, and the ceremony was followed by a banquet and a ball. Some twenty years later Rubens recalled this scene when he came to paint the life of Marie de Médicis for her new palace, the Luxembourg. In Florence, Rubens took the opportunity of studying the city's artistic treasures, and made a number of drawings after works of art, including the unfinished fresco of the Battle of Anghiari, proof that not all his time was spent in the duke's retinue. Even the hours of darkness were occupied by study, as is shown by the two copies after Michelangelo's youthful bas-relief of the *Battle of the Lapiths and Centaurs,* which he lit with a candle, first from one side and then from the other. Rubens remained in the service of Gonzaga for the next twelve months, though from a chance remark in a letter written to him by his brother Philip, who was also in Italy, it is clear that he was not kept in Mantua but had the opportunity to visit other towns, either in Vincenzo's retinue or alone.

The copy made by Rubens after Leonardo's unfinished fresco of the Battle of Anghiari
in the Palazzo Vecchio in Florence

The copy made by Rubens after Michelangelo's fresco, *The Creation of Eve*, on the ceiling of the Sistine Chapel

At the end of 1601 Rubens was at last given the chance to visit Rome. Gonzaga wrote to the influential Cardinal Montalto, a nephew of the pope, asking for his protection for the painter Peter Paul, who was coming to Rome to make copies of paintings, while he, Gonzaga, pursued war in Croatia. For Rubens this commission killed two birds with one stone. He was able to serve his master and at the same time further his study of Italian art in what was the most important living monument of the High Renaissance. But Rome was not only a museum of the art of the past. During the first four years of the new century a revival in activity took place with the arrival in Rome of the Carracci and Caravaggio, and their work was beginning to appear in the churches and palaces precisely at the moment that Rubens arrived. Unfortunately, we do not know whether the young artist actually met and talked with these artists, though it is clear from the copies he made of their works, and the effect they had on his own painting, that he was keenly interested. As well as studying, Rubens was given the chance of doing more creative work. The Archduke Albert, who before he married the

A preparatory study for *Christ crowned with thorns,* one of the three altarpieces painted in 1602 for S. Croce in Gerusalemme, Rome

daughter of Philip II had been a cardinal, wished to adorn with an altarpiece the Church of S. Croce in Gerusalemme, from which he had taken his cardinal's title. He wrote to his ambassador in Rome, asking him to find a suitable artist who would produce a worthy tribute. By one of those master-strokes of knowing the right person at the right time, which were to play such an important part in Rubens' life, his name was soon considered. On this occasion the connecting link was his brother Philip, who had acted as secretary to the ambassador's father, and who was now accompanying the ambassador's brother on a visit to Italy. As a result of this contact Rubens was commissioned to paint an altarpiece of Saint Helena discovering the true cross for the main altar in the chapel, and two other panels for the side altars.

*Philip Rubens*　　To enable him to finish this work Vincenzo de Gonzaga granted his artist several extra months in Rome, so that Rubens did not return to Mantua until April 1602. There he spent another year, though apart from a happy reunion with his brother Philip we do not know much about his movements. Deep affection existed between the two brothers, and Philip had written on his arrival in Italy that 'my first desire was to see Italy, my second to meet you there again; the first is fulfilled and the second will, I hope, soon be fulfilled.' Philip was an

18

Justus Lipsius with his two former pupils, Philip Rubens and Jan Woverius, with a self-portrait of Peter Paul Rubens on the far left

ardent classical scholar, who now, in addition to looking after the ambassador's brother, was engaged in reading for his degree of Doctor of Law at the university of Rome. The brothers must have shared their joy at discovering new and different facets of the country which was to be their spiritual home, and they must have stimulated each other with their different interests and standpoints. Rubens later painted a portrait of his brother and his friend Woverius, who was also in Italy, seated on either side of their former master, the distinguished professor of Louvain, Justus Lipsius, who discourses on a classical text. Behind the professor, a bust of Seneca alludes to Lipsius' celebrated edition of Seneca's writings, and on the far left the painter himself appears, spiritually of the company, even if he never had the honour of being a pupil. Ruins reminiscent of the Palatine give the key to where all their thoughts were turned.

Philip III on horseback
painted by Velazquez
after the king's death

Rubens was not allowed to remain inactive for long in Mantua. He must have impressed himself on the duke as a reliable person, suitable to send on a delicate diplomatic mission, and already the pattern of his life was taking shape. For a small state, to remain free and intact, surrounded as it was by larger powers only too ready to add it to their possessions, required considerable diplomacy as well as cunning and skill. Gonzaga showed himself ever ready to assuage the greed of the bigger powers by putting them in his debt. He was, for example, always prepared to march to war to support the emperor, or to lead his whole court to another city to do homage to the pope. On this occasion it was the turn of Spain to receive the ducal *douceur*. Apart from promises of general protection he particularly coveted the post of admiral, which had fallen vacant through the disgrace of its former holder, Giovanni Andrea Doria of Genoa. Gifts had already been sent to Philip III and his chief minister, the Duke of Lerma. Now further gifts were prepared to press home the advantage, and Rubens was chosen to accompany them to Spain and witness the presentation.

20

Rubens set off from Mantua in the early spring of 1603, with six chargers loaded on wagons – the presents included such bulky objects as a small coach with six bay horses – and in a series of letters addressed to the duke's secretary of state he gave a vivid account of the hazards of travel in those days, as well as allowing us some insight into the artist's character and personality. The route he followed was the most circuitous imaginable. After numerous delays and changes of plan he finally reached Pisa, where he was entertained by the Grand Duke Ferdinand of Tuscany. Innocent of Italian intrigue, he was surprised that his host should be fully acquainted with his identity and the purpose of his supposedly secret mission. 'Perhaps it is my simplicity', he wrote back to Mantua, 'which causes me such astonishment at things that are ordinary at court. Pardon me, and read, as a pastime, the report of a novice without experience.' Rubens had expected to go to Madrid, but on arriving in Spain he discovered that the court had moved to Valladolid, which he finally reached 'after twenty days of tiresome travel, through daily rains and violent winds', only to find that by then the court had moved on to Burgos. So there he remained, penniless. He was not expected by the duke's treacherous agent Iberti, who was at first all smiles and full of protestations of help. But very soon Iberti showed his fangs, and at the presentation of Gonzaga's gifts shortly after the court's return to Valladolid, Rubens was to be given a sharp taste of the spite and petty jealousy of diplomatic behaviour, which in later years he was to know so well. The duke had commanded Iberti to present Rubens to the king, yet when the presentation of the coach actually took place, Iberti without a word changed the arrangements, leaving Rubens a mere spectator in the crowd. This petty injustice piqued Rubens, and he could not refrain from complaining with dignity to Mantua, following it

A view of Valladolid where Rubens finally met the Spanish court

Landscape near Madrid from the engraving by Bolswert after Rubens' painting ▶

The preparatory study for the equestrian portrait of the Duke of Lerma, painted in Spain

up with another letter which was intended as an answer to the calumnies Iberti was no doubt sending back: 'I do not fear the slightest suspicion of carelessness or fraud; I can meet the first accusation with a certain experience of my services, and the second with pure innocence.' He was aware of his worth and the correctness of his behaviour, and within the prescribed rules he was ready to fight for himself. He never stooped to use the weapons of the other side but had a sincere belief in the triumph of justice. It took him thirty years to become disillusioned in this belief where political matters were concerned, by which time he had experienced the whole gamut of fickleness and viciousness of human behaviour. To Annibale Iberti he was indebted for his first lesson.

22

In Spain he received another more profound lesson – that the divine right of kings does not automatically confer absolute power. Weak, pleasure-loving Philip III was ruler in name only; the real power lay in the hands of his first minister, the Duke of Lerma. Rubens not only recognized where true power lay but was called on to serve it by painting, among other works, an equestrian portrait of Lerma, in order to show the world 'that the Duke is not less well served than His Majesty'. Even the detested Iberti could not conceal that the work was arousing great interest and admiration. For his master in Mantua something less narcissistic was required, and Rubens painted a series of court beauties to take back with him.

His journey to Spain also gave him his first opportunity to study the artistic situation there. He reported that he saw 'so many splendid works of Titian, of Raphael and others, which astonished me, both by their quality and quantity, in the king's palace, in the Escorial and elsewhere. But as for the moderns, there is nothing of any worth', he continued, with the contempt and impatience of a young man who knew his own mind. He did not mince his words when he castigated 'the incredible incompetence and carelessness of the painters here. . . . God keep me from resembling them in any way.' His prayer was answered.

23

Rubens reached Mantua at the beginning of 1604, a wiser and better-travelled man. More than that, he seems to have realized his own stature; he had a healthy opinion of his capabilities. From the young painter always at his master's command he had matured into a man who knew what he was best fitted for. A subtle change in the tone of his letters to Mantua indicates that leading a mission, albeit a small one, gave Rubens that confident feeling that the world was at his command, and not the reverse. He was no less loyal and ready to serve, but he did not wish his services to be wasted on menial tasks and did not hesitate to say so clearly, if politely. A firmness of intent and a conviction in the correctness of his own opinion underlie every letter. In addition, he had the gift not only of knowing his own mind, but of being able to make others agree with him. To a suggestion that from Spain he should go to France to paint a series of court beauties – an idea which a few months before he had positively favoured – he now pleaded that local painters should do it: 'Then I should not have to waste more time, travel, expenses, salaries (even the munificence of His Highness will not repay all this) upon works unworthy of me, and which anyone can do to the Duke's taste. . . . I beg him earnestly to employ me, at home or abroad, in works more appropriate to my talent.' The duke took him at his word, and on his return to Mantua commanded him to paint three large altarpieces for the Jesuit church, one of which, destined for the high altar, depicted the Trinity adored by the duke and his family. Rubens was at last carrying out 'works more appropriate to my talent.'

A fragment from the painting, *The Gonzaga family adoring the Trinity*, formerly in the Church of the Holy Trinity, executed during the artist's stay in Mantua

*The Ruins on the Palatine*, from the engraving by Bolswert after the painting by Rubens

Apart from the thought that must have gone into their preparation, the sheer size alone must have absorbed much of the artist's time and energies, so that it is hardly surprising that the constant traveller appears to have stayed put in Mantua for nearly two years.

By the end of 1605 Rubens escaped from Mantua and returned to Rome for what was the most interesting and rewarding part of his Italian journey. His brother Philip was already installed there as librarian to Cardinal Ascanio Colonna, so that they were able to live together in a house, waited upon by two servants, in the Strada della Croce, just near the Piazza di Spagna. The visit started off badly since Rubens was laid low with pleurisy. As soon as he had recovered, he 'devoted all the summer to the study of art'. He lived and breathed the atmosphere of the classical age and the Renaissance. With Philip he undertook an intensive survey of Roman antiquity, which bore fruit in a book on the customs of ancient Rome,

*Second visit to Rome*

One of the engraved illustrations from drawings prepared by the artist for his brother's book on classical antiquity

written by Philip and illustrated with engravings after drawings made by Peter Paul. Together they made a perfect combination, with Philip providing the scholarship and Peter Paul the artistic imagination. For the artist these were important months, which gave him a deep understanding of classical art and literature, so that in later years he was able to penetrate to the very heart of the classical subjects he was called upon to execute. It must have been an immensely pleasurable time, surrounded by kindred spirits all absorbed in a study of the *caput mundi*, with few of the nagging irritations of court life, apart from the constant non-payment of his salary. To his activities as scholar and artist he now added that of collector, and when he returned home to Antwerp he had already amassed a considerable number of sculptures. He was also able to renew acquaintance with living artists and eagerly absorbed their latest preoccupations. Caravaggio was about to flee from Rome under a cloud, but Rubens had lost none of his admiration for him, and when Caravaggio's altarpiece, the *Death of the Virgin*, painted for the Church of S. Maria della Scala, was rejected he stepped in and recommended that Gonzaga purchase it.

26

Philip Rubens, an engraving
after a design by his brother

But the pleasant summer turned to what at first was a joyless winter. Philip Rubens returned to Antwerp as their mother's health was already beginning to cause concern. Gonzaga's funds were further strained by the marriage of one of his sons, and Rubens' salary was more tardily paid than ever. But recognition of his talents came with the offer of an important commission. He proudly dictated a letter to his brother to send back to Mantua, 'when the finest and most splendid opportunity in all Rome presented itself, my ambition urged me to avail myself of the chance. It is the high altar of the New Church of the Priests of the Oratory, called S. Maria in Valicella – without doubt the most celebrated and frequented church in Rome today, situated in the centre of the city, and to be adorned by the combined efforts of all the most able painters in Italy.' Rubens had quickly found influential patrons in Rome, such as Cardinal Scipio Borghese, nephew of Sixtus V, and Cardinal Serra. In this instance his contact was a friend and fellow-Fleming, Jan van Hemelaer, librarian to a member of the Cesi family, who provided the money for the building and decoration of the church. On this occasion Rubens was not disposed to play down his triumph, 'obtained so gloriously, against the pretentions of all the leading painters of Rome', when he asked Mantua for additional leave. How Annibale Carracci, Guido Reni and other artists reacted to the success of a young foreigner is unfortunately left to the imagination.

27

*Genoa*    Rubens was granted six months' extension to his stay in Rome, but in the summer he was summoned back to Mantua. He was preceded by a letter to the duke from Cardinal Borghese, pleading for his speedy return so that he could complete the altarpiece for the Chiesa Nuova. Rubens was required to accompany his master on a visit to Genoa, a city which he had probably not visited before. There they spent the summer months. For the artist it was not the waste of time that an official court visit might have been, and as well as painting a number of portraits of the exclusive Genoese aristocracy, he turned to an intensive study of architecture in the city. He collected plans and elevations of many of the palaces, which later, on his return to Antwerp, he had engraved and published as a book. It included a eulogy by him on architecture based on classical proportions in contrast to the 'barbarous or gothic architecture' found in the Low Countries.

At the end of August Gonzaga left Genoa and Rubens was permitted to return to Rome. His last stay in the city lacked the serenity of the previous summer, and he was beset by numerous worries and anxieties. News of his mother was not encouraging, and Archduke Albert unsuccessfully interceded with Gonzaga for his return. Constant irritants were Gonzaga's demands for him to return to Mantua, and his failure to pay his salary. By the turn of 1608 the great altarpiece was at last finished, and was praised and admired by all those responsible for the commission, 'which', as Rubens was already aware, 'rarely happens'. The final act of putting the altarpiece in place, however, turned success into tragedy.

A Genoese palace from the artist's book, *Palazzi di Genova*, published in 1622 and based on his visit to the city in 1607

28

The first unsuccessful version of the altarpiece painted for the Chiesa Nuova, Rome, which was later placed over his mother's tomb. (*right*) The oil sketch for the second version of the altarpiece which was painted on slate to avoid reflection

Owing to the fall of the light the picture was largely invisible. 'All the merit in the work is thrown away', and Rubens realized he could do nothing but remove it, no doubt to the accompaniment of malicious comments by some Italians, and replace it with another version, painted on slate. He did not rest content with making a faithful copy but completely altered the composition, dividing it up into three entirely different sections. Whereas a weaker man might have despaired, Rubens was prepared to put a brave face on it, and his last months in Rome were occupied with this task. He consoled himself with the thought that another purchaser might be found for the first version, and not without justification turned to Gonzaga who, he was only too keenly aware, after seven years possessed no major work of his, though pious wishes were not lacking. The duke, however, was not disposed to accept – a decision which must have confirmed Rubens' presentiment that as far as he was concerned the duke preferred painters to paintings.

When an urgent call came in the autumn for Rubens to return home as quickly as possible because his mother was dying, he cannot have felt any deep regret in leaving the service of the House of Gonzaga. At least he left of his own accord and was not ignominiously dismissed like Monteverdi after twenty years' devoted service. Rubens wrote in haste 'mounting horseback' to ask permission for leave of absence, though in fact he was taking it. The relationship had served its purpose for both parties, and there were no expressions of regret on either side, apart from Rubens' good manners. He had probably been contemplating a visit home for the whole summer and was held up only by the necessity of finishing the second version of the Chiesa Nuova altarpiece. Quite apart from his anxiety about his mother's health, he was now a mature man of thirty-one and most likely felt that it was time to settle. Though he did not lack patrons or commissions in Rome, he must have sensed that as the servant of Gonzaga he was only a visitor on a prolonged stay. Any uncertainty about his future plans was cut short by the summons home. Fate was making up his mind for him.

His haste was in vain. His mother had died nine days before he left Rome, and he arrived home to find her buried in the Abbey of St Michael, not far from the house in the Kloosterstraat where she had lived. To make amends for his absence from her deathbed, he had an altar constructed in the chapel where she was buried, and above it placed the first version of the altarpiece he had painted for the Chiesa Nuova. The painter himself described it as 'the best and most successful work I have ever done', an opinion in which his mother would have wholeheartedly concurred, and it was fitting that her memory should have been honoured with the fruit of the time spent in Italy, to which she so unselfishly had agreed. Rubens must have spent many enjoyable hours with his brother, as well as renewing acquaintance with his old friends in Antwerp. To compensate for the family grief at the death of Maria Pypelinx, a happier event in the shape of Philip's marriage took place in the following year in the spring. In an effusive moment, Rubens wrote to a friend in Rome that 'In short my brother has been favoured by Venus, the Cupids, Juno and all the gods; there has fallen to his lot a mistress who is beautiful, learned, gracious, wealthy and well-born, and alone able to refute the entire Sixth Satire of Juvenal.' More to the point were his own plans. He found himself at the crossroads, 'I have not yet made up my mind whether to remain in my own country or to return forever to Rome, where I am invited on the most favourable terms. Here also they do not fail to make every effort to keep me, by every sort of compliment. The Archduke and the Most Serene Infanta have had letters written urging me to remain in their service. Their offers are very generous, but I have little desire to become a courtier again. Antwerp and its citizens would satisfy me, if I could say farewell to Rome.'

The rub lay in the last phrase; Rome provided all that was congenial in artistic interest and companionship with none of the stranglehold of court life. He could not refrain from sending warm greetings to 'my friends whose good conversation makes me often long for Rome'. Rubens was paying the price for the fame and

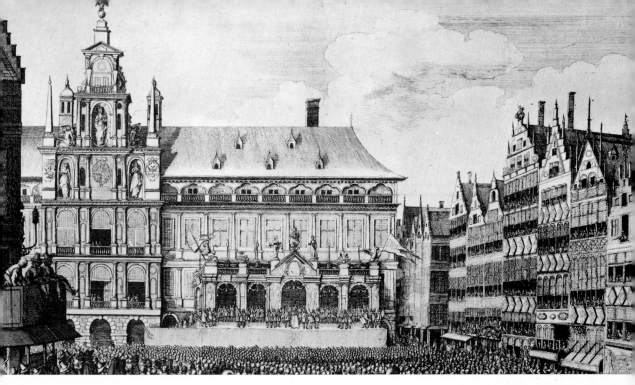

The town hall and market place in Antwerp

popularity which had preceded him back to his home country. Once again he was overtaken by events, and he rapidly found himself established in Antwerp by his sheer necessity to the city and to the court. As he mounted his horse in Rome he may have had a presentiment that he was saying a double farewell – to carefree days and to Italy. The latter was never far from his thoughts or his painting, and throughout his life it remained the Mecca of his dreams. Twenty years later he could write from the bottom of his heart: 'I have not given up hope of fulfilling my wish to go to Italy. In fact this desire grows from day to day, and I declare that if Fortune does not grant it, I shall neither live nor die content.' Even if Fortune did not grant it, she made generous amends.

So much was Rubens the painter of Antwerp, giving glory to its name, that it is an automatic reaction to suppose that the fecundity and well-being of the man reflect similar qualities in the city. It comes as a shock to learn that while Rubens was climbing to the very height of success, the city of Antwerp, which had been the greatest port and richest city in northern Europe in the sixteenth century, was fully embarked on its decline and fall. What Antwerp had been in the sixteenth century, Amsterdam became in the seventeenth. Antwerp had suffered heavily both psychologically and physically in the war between Spain and the northern Netherlands. Whereas the latter expressed all the youthful energy of a new nation, Flanders was weakened by the split and still bowed under the Spanish yoke. It

*Antwerp*

31

became the real victim of the civil war, and the deepest wound was the blocking of the Scheldt by the Dutch, which totally closed the port of Antwerp. Rubens' return almost coincided with the signing of the Twelve Years' Truce with the United Provinces. This should have ended the city's misery, but whereas Rubens flourished, the city sadly languished.

Sir Dudley Carleton, the English ambassador in The Hague, with whom Rubens was to have close relations, visited Antwerp in 1616; he wrote, 'it exceeds any I ever saw anywhere else for the beauty and uniformity of its buildings, the height and width of its streets, the strength and fairness of its ramparts', but 'the whole time we spent there I could never set my eyes in the whole length of a street upon forty persons at once: I never met coach nor saw man on horseback, none of our company saw one penny worth of ware either in the shops or in the streets bought or sold . . . in many places grass grows in the streets, yet (that which is rare in such solitariness) the buildings are kept in perfect repair.' Carleton rightly concluded that Antwerp's 'condition is much worse since the truce than before it'. And the situation got no better; years later Rubens himself wrote that 'this city, at least, languishes like a consumptive body, declining little by little. Every day sees a decrease in the number of inhabitants, for these unhappy people have no means of supporting themselves either by industrial skill or by trade.'

*Appointment as court painter*

One of the most attractive features of Rubens, and indeed one which contributed so enormously to his general happiness of life, was his self-knowledge. He knew his worth and was prepared to argue on that basis. He was ambitious, but he was not prepared to sell his soul to achieve his aspirations. If he stayed in Antwerp, one of the decisions he had to face was whether to accept Albert and Isabella's offer to become court painter. He had already tasted court life in Audenarde, Mantua and Spain, and he knew full well how much he disliked the stultifying, petty atmosphere that almost invariably surrounds a close circle centred round an autocrat. As he himself said, 'I have little desire to become a courtier again.' In a truly modern way he wished for freedom of thought and action. Something of this was realized by Albert and Isabella, for in accepting their offer of court painter Rubens was accepting no more than the title and honour. First and foremost, he was absolved from the necessity of living in the court at Brussels, and could pursue his life as a free man in Antwerp. His post entailed no duties, and any works carried out for the archducal pair were paid for separately. All in all he was gaining honour and advantage without loss of freedom. It was an appropriate beginning in the artist's very special relationship with the archduke, and, above all, with his wife, which deepened through the years.

Rubens' new patrons were no upstarts in European aristocracy. Albert was the son of the Emperor Maximilian, while Isabella was the daughter of Philip II of Spain and the apple of his eye as well. With Isabella's hand went the sovereignty of the Netherlands, but the gift was hedged with conditions that made its return to Spain only too probable. Moreover, though entitled to rule as sovereigns, Albert and Isabella had to suffer considerable interference and pressure from the

Archduke Albert and Archduchess Isabella; probably the artist's first portraits of his new patrons

Spaniards. Like others of that name, Albert was a dutiful husband and a worthy and upright man. In common with other rulers of seventeenth-century Europe, he was a great admirer of the fine arts and owned a large collection of pictures. He was ready to honour artists, and, apart from Rubens, Jan Bruegel and Otto van Veen were also granted the title of court painter. His wife was also a person of calibre, but her true personality only came to light in later years after her husband's death, when Rubens was there to see and admire it – and to serve her.

In Antwerp he at first lived with his brother Philip, who in 1609 became *Marriage* secretary of the city, in their mother's house in the Kloosterstraat, near the Steen and the harbour. Philip was the first to leave when he married, and in spite of Peter Paul's firm declaration that 'I will not dare to follow him, for he has made such a good choice that it seems inimitable,' his brother's example, as so often happens with close friends and relations, was simulated only a few months later, even to the extent of choosing a member of the same family. The younger brother fell in love with the niece of his sister-in-law and led her to the altar in October 1609 in the Abbey of St Michael, where his mother was buried. Since this was not a parish church and the marriage was registered elsewhere, it is clear that filial

33

Self-portrait with Isabella Brant in a bower of honeysuckle, painted shortly after their marriage ▶

Jan Brant, the artist's first father-in-law (detail)

piety prompted this special arrangement. Isabella Brant, born in 1591, was the eldest daughter of Jan Brant, who, in company with Philip Rubens, was one of the four secretaries of Antwerp, and whose wife's sister Philip married. He was well educated and, like many public servants of those days, pursued academic learning as a pastime. Jan Brant's chosen field of Sunday study was classical literature, and he published, among other works, notes on Julius Caesar. There is something appealing in his vigorous high-coloured face, which gives an impression of bluffness, though not lacking in sensitivity. His relationship with Rubens was not confined to that of father- and son-in-law, and a true friendship existed between them, so that contact was maintained long after Isabella's death. His eldest daughter, like so many women of the time, remains a far more shadowy figure. The only description of her is her husband's own tributes on her death, when he wrote of her as 'an excellent companion, whom one could love – indeed had to love with good reason – as having none of the faults of her sex. She had no capricious moods, and no feminine weaknesses, but was all goodness and honesty. And because of her virtues she was loved during her lifetime, and mourned by all at her death.'

The double portrait, probably painted in the year of their marriage, possibly to record the event, sets the tone of their partnership. In a bower of honeysuckle Isabella, dressed in all her finery, sits at Rubens' feet, her hand resting affectionately on her husband's, while she looks a little shyly out at us. As a good wife she was clearly ready to serve her husband, but there was nothing hesitant or formal about their relationship. Though in perfect harmony with Rubens, her own personality was to remain intact, and she never became subservient to her husband's opinions.

The happiness of a successful marriage promised here was later confirmed in an intimate drawing, made shortly before her death, when the girlish charm of the double portrait has been exchanged for a fuller, maturer face with plump cheeks. She is now attractive by virtue of her personality rather than her actual looks. Her eyes sparkle with vitality, and she cannot resist breaking into a gay smile, giving her large dimples, as she lovingly looks directly at her husband drawing her. Such an intimate and vivacious portrait can only have been the result of perfect happiness after many years of marriage. For a serious young man, already with a great reputation, she must have been the perfect, steadfast companion as they marched straight ahead, like Tamino and Pamina, *Mann und Weib und Weib und Mann.*

*Their house*    After their marriage they went to live in her father's house in the same street, but this was intended only as a temporary arrangement while they looked around for a house suitable both in size and in status. By the end of 1610 Rubens had found what he wanted. He bought a large house with an extensive garden on the Wapper, a canal formerly part of the moat of the old fortifications of the city, near the fashionable square of the Meir. Even if very expensive, it was an admirable purchase because it gave the Rubens family extensive accommodation with sufficient space for further building. Though he specifically disclaimed any intention of living like a prince, the scale and style of his house and possessions

Bird's-eye view of Antwerp; from the commemorative volume of the *Introitus Ferdinandi* published in 1635. The artist's house on the Wapper is situated within the marked circle

The courtyard of the artist's house looking through the triumphal arch towards the garden; the old laundry on the left, and the artist's new studio on the right

The garden of the artist's house with the end of the studio on the right and the garden pavilion on the left

were nevertheless in many ways a smaller version of some of the Italian courts he had seen and lived in. The existing building, a typical sixteenth-century Flemish house, consisted of a wide front facing the street, with an additional wing at the back of the building, bordering the courtyard, which had been used as a laundry. At the back there was also a garden which adjoined the premises of the Guild of Arquebusiers. As it stood, the property was not sufficient for the artist, and on the other side of the courtyard over the course of the next decade he built a large studio with a smaller one at the back. Closing the courtyard on the garden side, Rubens erected a triumphal arch. Both the façade and the arch were designed in a rich baroque style, inspired by the architecture he had seen in Italy, above all in Mantua and Genoa. The lower part of the façade of the studio was decorated with sculpture and grisailles simulating marble reliefs. On the triumphal arch carved reliefs were placed in spandrels, and above each arch was a sculpted bust. Finally, at the end of the garden, he built a small pavilion decorated once again with sculpture on classical themes. The garden itself was divided up into beds filled with flowers and surrounded by small hedges. As in Italian gardens, small trees in pots were placed at various points. For an unwilling exile from Italy, Rubens' house and garden provided as much consolation as can be obtained in a northern climate.

The interior of a contemporary Antwerp house, sometimes supposed to be Rubens', with his collection of sculpture in the right-hand background

Sir Dudley Carleton, the English ambassador at The Hague, a detail from a painting showing him in attendance on the Countess of Arundel

Rubens further embellished his property by building a semicircular room, lit by a lantern from above, in emulation of classical architecture, at the back of what was originally the laundry. Around the wall were niches for classical sculpture. Already in Italy Rubens had started to collect, but his major acquisitions in this field came through an exchange effected with Sir Dudley Carleton. Fortunately, most of his correspondence relating to this deal exists and allows us to watch Rubens as an honest, straightforward, but hard bargainer. 'I like to be correct in my affairs, and to give full satisfaction to everyone.' The affair opened almost casually with Carleton's agent being sent to Antwerp to try to exchange a diamond necklace for a hunting piece by Rubens, but the latter valued his picture more highly than the necklace and was not prepared to reduce the price on his work. As the same agent put it on a later occasion, 'his demands are like the laws of the Medes and Persians which may not be altered.'

This was only the first salvo in their relationship, and in 1618 Rubens wrote to Carleton about the latter's 'rare collection of antiquities', which he had heard Carleton was prepared to exchange for pictures by his hand. It was a curious deal since neither side actually saw what the other was offering, even though at one point Carleton suggested that Rubens should visit him 'before proceeding with our business so that you may avoid buying a pig in a poke as they say.' For his part, Rubens drew up a list of pictures he had in stock, stating whether they were entirely by his hand or done with the assistance of pupils. Though describing the

*Deal with Carleton*

39

goods honestly and accurately, Rubens was not averse to a little sales talk *pour encourager*, 'I find that at present I have in the house the flower of my stock, particularly some pictures which I have kept for my own enjoyment.' For his part, Carleton was to say what his collection had cost him; 'In regard to this I wish to place complete trust in your knightly word. I am also to believe that you made such purchases with all judgment and prudence, although', Rubens added shrewdly, 'high personages, in buying or selling, are sometimes likely to have a certain disadvantage, because many people are willing to compute the price of goods by the rank of the purchaser – a practice to which I am very averse.' After some gentlemanly but hard bargaining, the deal was concluded, and as Rubens somewhat one-sidedly put it to Carleton, 'in exchange for marbles to furnish one room' (namely twenty-one large statues, eight statues of children, four torsos, fifty-seven heads of various sizes, seventeen pedestals, five urns, four bas-reliefs and eighteen busts of Roman emperors!) 'Your Excellency receives pictures to adorn an entire palace.'

A preparatory study for *Daniel in the lion's den*, one of the paintings given to Carleton in exchange for his collection of antique statuary; Carleton later gave the painting to Charles I

Nicolaas Rockox and his wife, from the wings of the altarpiece he commissioned from Rubens for the Church of the Recollects

Rubens was immediately a success, both professionally and socially, in his home town, as well as at the court at Brussels. Never has anyone had to strive less for recognition. The leading men of Antwerp were only too honoured to count him among their friends, and no doubt his brother Philip had blazed the trail. His friendly contacts with the establishment of Antwerp quickly led to important commissions for paintings. Where other great artists were often too awkward and uncompromising to achieve harmonious relationships with those in power, Rubens had not only the social manners, but, unlike so many of the establishment's chosen artists, the artistic greatness to do full justice to the commissions.

Typical of the artist's Antwerp friends was Nicolaas Rockox, burgomaster of the

A view of Rockox's dining-room by Frans Francken the Younger, showing Rubens' painting of *Samson and Delilah* hanging over the fireplace

city, and also chief of the Guild of Arquebusiers whose quarters were adjacent to his garden. The two men had much in common. Rubens himself described Rockox as 'an honest man and a connoisseur of antiquities, a good administrator, and all in all a gentleman of the most blameless reputation'. As was natural, their friend-ship brought Rubens a number of public and private commissions. One of their earliest contacts was the order for a painting for the Town Hall, which Rubens executed shortly after his return to Antwerp. Personal commissions followed in the shape of a *Crucifixion* and a *Samson and Delilah*; the latter can be seen hanging over the fireplace in the painting of a room in Rockox's house. But more important commissions were to come through the latter's influence.

The preparatory study for the painting of *Samson and Delilah*

Undoubtedly Rockox's position as chief of the Guild of Arquebusiers was partly instrumental in the request for an altarpiece from Rubens for the Guild's chapel in the Church of Notre-Dame. Rubens had already shown his abilities in the triptych of the *Raising of the Cross*, painted for the Church of St Walburga, and now he agreed to execute a triptych on the same scale, the *Descent from the Cross*. The altarpiece clearly pleased Rockox, who celebrated the occasion by ordering another smaller triptych for himself, to be hung in the Church of the Recollects over the altar where the tomb of his wife and himself was to be placed. Some years later Rockox further adorned the Church of the Recollects by asking Rubens to paint the *Coup de Lance* for the high altar.

43

Rubens' second design for the printer's mark of the
Plantin press, made about 1635 for Balthasar Moretus

Rubens' design for the title-page of Justus Lipsius'
edition of the works of Seneca published by the
Plantin press in 1615

Other friendships led to other commissions, sometimes of a slightly different
nature. Balthasar Moretus, one of his earliest friends from Verdonck's school, was
the grandson of Christopher Plantin, and in due course he took over the press.
His house was as grand as Rubens', and their mutual friend, Jan Woverius, the
town clerk, wrote that 'their houses will evoke the astonishment of visitors as well
as admiration'. Friendship and business went hand in hand, and in no time
Rubens was working for the Plantin press, painting portraits and designing title-
pages and illustrations, most notably those to the Roman Breviary. One task that
he must have done with particular pleasure was to design a title-page with a
portrait for Justus Lipsius' edition of the works of Seneca. The bust of Seneca,
it will be remembered, had appeared behind Lipsius in the commemorative
portrait Rubens had painted of him with Philip Rubens, Woverius and himself.

More surprisingly, in view of the mutual jealousy among artists, he met with
immediate success within his own profession. He was welcomed at a special
banquet given in his honour by Jan Bruegel, the dean of the Romanists, a
society for artists and intellectuals of which Rubens himself was shortly to
become dean. With Jan Bruegel, who had been to Italy, he formed a close friendship, and not only did they work together on certain pictures, but Rubens found
time to act as the older man's amanuensis in his Italian correspondence, since
Bruegel did not know the language. Rubens' success can be gauged above all

◀ The central panel from the altarpiece of the *Descent
from the Cross* painted for the Guild of Arquebusiers for
their chapel in Notre-Dame, and now in the Cathedral

45

by the popularity of his studio. Only two years after his return, he wrote, 'From all sides applications reach me. Some young men remain here for several years with other masters, awaiting a vacancy in my studio. Among others, my friend, and (as you know) patron M. Rockox, has only with great difficulty obtained a place for a youth whom he himself brought up and whom, in the meantime, he was having trained by others. I can tell you truly, without exaggeration, that I have to refuse over one hundred, even some of my own relatives or my wife's, and not without causing great displeasure among many of my best friends.'

In no time Rubens had a large studio of assistants and pupils, whose help was *The artist's* increasingly necessary as the number and scale of commissions grew. Sometimes *studio* he collaborated with other artists – for example, Jan Bruegel and Jan Wildens. The former would be responsible for garlands of flowers or other still-life details, while the latter would be given the landscape to paint. Rubens himself would confine his contribution to the figures. In his dealings with patrons he made a clear distinction between 'an original by my hand' and 'original by my hand except a most beautiful landscape, done by the hand of a master skilful in that department', or copies done by pupils and then 'so well retouched by my hand that they are hardly to be distinguished from originals'. But if he did make a distinction between the different categories and priced them accordingly, he signed himself responsible for everything that left the studio.

By the middle of his career he was firmly of the opinion 'that I am, by natural instinct, better fitted to execute very large works than small curiosities. Everyone according to his gifts; my talent is such that no undertaking however vast in size or diversified in subject has ever surpassed my courage.' And to realize these projects he needed the help of others. A visitor described seeing 'a large hall which had no windows but was lighted through an opening in the ceiling. In this hall were a number of young painters: all at work on different pictures, for which Rubens had made the drawings in chalks indicating the tones here and there which Rubens would afterwards finish himself. The work would then pass for a Rubens.' By far his most distinguished assistant was van Dyck, some twenty-two years younger than the master. He had already been trained by another artist at an early age, and by the time he was nineteen Rubens was referring to him as 'the best of my pupils'. Rubens made the most of his help during the short time he worked for him. In 1620, seeing little future in Antwerp, van Dyck went off to London.

The age of the large studio reached its height in the seventeenth century with Bernini in Rome, Lebrun at Versailles and Rubens in Antwerp, each of whom employed a team of artists to realize their grandiose projects. In the scale and abundance of decorative schemes, Rubens was very much a man of his time, and in running this thriving factory he showed himself a superb administrator. But the Rubens studio was more than a collection of pupils and assistants. It was concerned with spreading the name of the master, and one of the most important methods was the publication of engravings and woodcuts after pictures. Rubens' interest was such that he would often make a drawing or painting in scale for the

◀ Self-portrait by Van Dyck at about the age of fifteen

Self-portrait at about
the age of thirty-eight ▶

Rubens' engraver,
Lucas Vorsterman,
from a drawing by
Van Dyck (detail)

engraver to follow. Frequently, when shown the first pulls of a print, he would correct it himself with his pen or brush in order that nothing should be left to chance when the engraver completed the work. Such was the general interest in Rubens' works that he was forced to patent his designs in order to stop other engravers from issuing them. His troubles over prints were not only confined to the works themselves. In 1618 he had found an excellent printmaker, Lucas Vorsterman, with whom he worked most profitably and harmoniously; but four years later Rubens lamented that 'unfortunately we have made almost nothing for a couple of years, due to the caprices of my engraver who has to let himself sink into a dead calm, so that I can no longer deal with him or come to an understanding with him. He contends that it is his engraving alone and his illustrious name that give these prints any value.' In his megalomania Vorsterman even threatened Rubens with his life and the master had to be given protection. In coping with the engraver's mental breakdown, Rubens was facing the human problems of the employer, and he was made keenly aware that art was a down-to-earth business not practised in the solitude of an ivory tower.

48

Rubens' productivity was not entirely due to the organization of his studio. He himself had a fertility and speed of thought and execution that were largely responsible for his astonishing output. Bellori graphically referred to his *furia del pennello*. His energy and powers of concentration greatly impressed a young Dane who visited him and wrote a somewhat fanciful description of 'the great artist at work. While still painting, he was having Tacitus read aloud to him and was dictating a letter. When we kept silent so as not to disturb him with our talk, he himself began to talk to us while still continuing to work, to listen to the reading and to dictate his letter, answering our questions and thus displaying his astonishing powers.' Though such Herculean powers of concentration may have been beyond even Rubens, the atmosphere of hectic activity is certainly correct in essence. A far more convincingly life-like portrait of the artist at work was given by a visiting Englishman: 'Usually Rubens would (with his Arms a cross) sit musing upon his work for some time, and in an instant in the liveliness of spirit, with a nimble hand, would force out his overcharged brain into description so as not to be contained in the Compass of ordinary practice, but by a violent driving on of the passion. The Commotions of the mind, are not to be cooled by slow performance.' This bursting energy is vividly suggested by many of his paintings or drawings in which the brushstrokes and the penlines convey the speed of execution. Rubens was not the kind of artist to ruminate for hours before an unfinished canvas and then put it away untouched to wait for another more favourable day. Determination to complete the work in hand drove him on to a solution there and then. He often changed his mind, as different sketches for the same work show, but each work had an absolute conviction, as if it were to be the final result. There was no uncertain fumbling towards a yet unrealized goal.

*Character*    A similarly unromantic attitude seems to have underlain Rubens the man. It is hard to know whether he was ever faced with soul-searching moments in his life, since his response to every problem or event appears to have been one of action, and not of reflection inspired by doubt. His life is a shining example of the *vita activa*. Above the archway leading into his garden were inscribed the words, *mens sana in corpore sano*, and their message was taken as a guiding principle by the artist. But one is led to wonder whether his belief in himself, in his art, and in his religion could have been as uncomplicated as it appears. Was such an exemplary life achieved with so little apparent struggle? As we know him today, he stands apart from the rest of humanity as a very great man almost without any dark corners in his make-up. Anyone with a healthy cynicism towards perfection in human nature must come to this conclusion reluctantly, but before accusing Rubens of lacking finer feelings, one should remember that his activities in other spheres made him a highly sophisticated man, with a protective public image, behind which it is difficult to penetrate. With a few exceptions, letters of a more personal nature no longer survive, and we have to accept the fact that we cannot know the private man. Behind the cool judgments and reactions, a man of deep emotions and contradictions, frequently gnawed by human doubt, may

One of the letters written by Rubens to Sir Dudley Carleton; detail showing the date and signature

have existed. Yet it is no less conceivable that, had one had the opportunity to know him intimately, one would have discovered that the deeds of his life were the whole person, and that our understanding of the man is not impaired by the relative lack of personal records.

Ambition was undoubtedly a driving force in Rubens' career but if it was initially inspired by self-seeking, it was very soon directed towards entirely worthy causes. Though he had a very healthy opinion of himself and his works, he never succumbed to conceit and self-satisfaction. In financial matters, he was hard-headed and calculating, charging according to the day's work. He seemed to approach each project as a job to be executed with the maximum efficiency. Like a craftsman he never appears to have been becalmed for want of inspiration. But he was not in the final resort grasping, and if he charged accordingly, it was because the 'labourer is worthy of his hire'. When under pressure he showed a natural impatience, and he did not suffer fools gladly. But these are peccadilloes to be set against the positive good in his character, and we are filled with admiration for his noble sentiments and actions, his extensive and deep knowledge, his generosity, his shrewdness about human nature. He was, for example, unwilling to believe ill of someone without making his own investigation: 'I do not want to rely upon public gossip, to the detriment of so illustrious a man. I shall visit him at home, and talk with him intimately, if possible.' In smaller, more everyday matters, he showed himself keenly aware of human behaviour: 'this book which I brought recently from Paris, upon your suggestion, pleased me so much that I did not want to enjoy alone the satisfaction it gave me, and so I lent it to an intimate friend. I have never been able to get it back, which will make me more careful about lending books in the future.'

Rubens put his finger firmly on the nature of his character when he declared: 'As for me, I assure you that in public affairs I am the most dispassionate man in the world, except where my property and person are concerned.' Detachment allowed him a very objective view of the world at large. He was doubtless right when he claimed that he 'could provide an historian with much material, and the pure truth of the case, very different from that which is generally believed.' Unfettered by self-interest and *parti pris*, he could see the world in a colder more accurate light. Moreover, his aloof position was protected by his continuing

The interior of the Jesuit church in Antwerp, showing Rubens' decorations in the vaults of the aisles and his painting over the high altar

The preparatory sketch of *St Cecilia*, one of the ceiling decorations in the Jesuit church

reluctance to get involved in the in-fighting of everyday political life. He formulated his creed and he kept to it: 'I am a peace-loving man, and I abhor chicanery like the plague, as well as every sort of dissension. I believe that it ought to be the wish of every honest man to live in tranquillity of mind, publicly and in private, rendering service to many and injurying no one.' For a man of his century, peace was an obsession, in whose cause he never ceased to fight. All his diplomatic activities were directed towards the cessation of hostilities and an honourable truce. That represented the ideal for which he fought, and never for personal aggrandizement or national glory.

By the end of the second decade of the century Rubens was a name to conjure with, not only in his home country but increasingly throughout Europe. Commissions were pouring in from all quarters. He had reached a halfway stage between his report of 1614 that 'I am at present charged with more great works than I have ever had' and his *cri de cœur* in 1625 that 'I am the busiest and most harassed man in the world.' Overtures were being made by Charles I, then Prince of Wales, and Rubens was also in contact with the Duke of Neuberg. He had not neglected his home town meanwhile, and in the course of ten years had decorated numerous churches and private houses with his works. It is largely paintings of this period that the visitor sees there today. Before losing Rubens, his home town seized the opportunity to commission him for one major scheme of decoration, which, alas, no longer exists. The Jesuits in their heyday of expansion had just completed a sumptuous new church in Antwerp. Its crowning splendour was thirty-nine ceiling paintings by Rubens, which, in the words of his friend Woverius, 'represent side by side the mysteries of religion drawn from the Old and New Testament, or else celebrated saints of both sexes,' as well as two large canvases of the miracles of the two Jesuit saints, St Ignatius Loyola and

*The Jesuit church*

53

One of the artist's designs for carved reliefs on the façade of the Jesuit church

St Francis Xavier. Rubens had contracted in March 1620 to supply these works by the end of that year. He himself was to make the sketches, while the paintings were to be executed in his studio, in the main by van Dyck, who was then 'the crown prince'. In addition he made a number of drawings for sculpture on the façade and several designs for the interior, such as a design for the high altar and for the ceiling of the Lady Chapel. The decoration of the church was a project in which Rubens became deeply involved, and it is hardly surprising that the result met with his approval. It was the first really large scheme that his studio had undertaken, and it was a triumphant success. Woverius was not found lacking in enthusiasm, and in a descriptive booklet, published by their mutual friend Moretus at the Plantin press, he wrote, 'The magnificence of the interior of the edifice turns the thoughts to the abode of heaven.' He had formulated the ethos of religious baroque art, and Rubens could ask for no better apologist.

When a scheme of decoration for the newly built Banqueting House in Whitehall was mooted to Rubens by James I's agent in Brussels, Rubens replied: 'I am by natural instinct better fitted to execute very large works.' This was no empty boast since the previous day he had attended the consecration of the Jesuit church. A few months later he was to be taken at his word, not by the English court, but by Marie de Médicis, widow of Henry IV of France, whose proxy marriage he had attended as a young man in Florence. In January 1622 he was called to Paris to discuss projects for the decoration of the Luxembourg Palace. Marie de Médicis, after a brief and quarrelsome marriage that had abruptly ended with her husband's assassination, had continued to reign as regent until her son Louis XIII came of age. The new king soon quarrelled with his mother, and banished her for a few years in the wilderness. She was allowed to return to Paris largely through the skilful intervention of the then unknown Abbé de Luçon, later Cardinal Richelieu, and occupied herself with building a large palace designed by Salomon de Brosse on the site of the *hôtel* of the Duke of Luxembourg. Like her ancestors, she was prepared to play the patron of the arts in a big way, and part of the scheme of decoration was to consist of two series of paintings to adorn two large galleries; one cycle was to illustrate events from her own life, the other that of her late husband.

The garden front of the Luxembourg Palace, built by Salomon de Brosse for Marie de Médicis, from an engraving by Israel Silvestre

A view of the Pont-Neuf from an etching by Callot (detail). Rubens stayed near here

*The Médicis series*    The queen's adviser, the Abbé de Saint-Ambroise, had publicly declared that 'two painters of Italy would not carry out in ten years what Rubens would do in four, and would not even think of undertaking pictures of the necessary size'. Rubens' name was now well known in the courts of Europe, and any necessary encouragement to entrust him with such a task would have been supplied by Marie de Médicis' friend and Rubens' patron, the Archduchess Isabella. When the artist went to Paris to discuss the project he bore gifts of a small dog and a necklace from Isabella to the French queen mother. The discussion lasted six weeks, during which time Rubens stayed on the Quai Saint-Germain l'Auxerrois, just near the Pont-Neuf. He then returned to Antwerp with a signed contract to decorate the two galleries for the sum of twenty thousand crowns, and he set to work on what was the most diplomatic undertaking of his artistic career. The subject-matter of the Jesuit church cycle had presented no problems, but when he turned to the inglorious career of Marie de Médicis, considerable imagination, aided by an abundant use of classical allegory, was necessary to present the

56

Portrait study of Marie de Médicis done from life for the *Majority of Louis XIII* in the Médicis series (detail)

quarrelsome heroine as the embodiment of all the virtues. Rubens was equal to the task, and he played an important part in drawing up the incidents to be illustrated, taking great care to avoid contentious issues, such as any reference to the murder of her husband. The final result was an elaborate and skilful masque, which covered up the true facts of history. On almost every occasion the heroine is attended by goddesses, sirens, angels and *putti*, useful for diverting and giving substance to purely static and uneventful scenes, such as her arrival at Marseilles or the birth of her son. It is a most glorious pageant which testifies to the richness of Rubens' imagination. And yet this sophisticated decorative scheme did not come entirely from the artist's mind. The queen mother herself was studied from life in several chalk drawings. Even the attendant figures were not entirely divorced from everyday reality, since at one point Rubens wrote from Antwerp asking for 'the two Capaio ladies of the Rue du Verbois, and also the little niece Louysa. For I intend to make three studies of sirens in life-size, and these three persons will be of infinitely great help to me, partly because of the wonderful expression of their faces, but even more by their superb black hair, which I find it difficult to obtain elsewhere, and also by their stature.'

57

*Marriage of Marie de Médicis* from the Médicis series

*Landing of Marie de Médicis at Marseilles* from the Médicis series

Cardinal Richelieu from the triple portrait executed by Philippe de Champaigne, to be sent to a sculptor as a model possibly for a portrait bust

By dint of hard work and the neglect of other people's commissions, the first cycle was finished in 1625. Though the paintings were admired, Rubens was already the victim of political manœuvres and personal jealousies. 'I am somewhat concerned about my own personal affairs. . . . I cannot make any requests without incurring the blame of fatiguing the queen with private matters.' Though he was kept away from Marie de Médicis, he consoled himself with the reflection that 'I am certain that the queen mother is very satisfied with my work, as she has many times told me so with her own lips, and has also repeated it to everyone.' Apart from the natural jealousies of certain courtiers and French artists, the prime cause of Rubens' disenchantment with the French court was none other than Richelieu. In the four years that Rubens had taken to execute the first part of the commission the cardinal had risen rapidly and become all-powerful. By now he had begun to recognize Rubens as a political adversary, and as the quarrel between Richelieu and the queen mother intensified, so the dislike between the two men increased. The favourable impression Rubens had of Richelieu when they first met rapidly deteriorated, and nearly ten years later in a rare bout of righteous anger at the news of the queen mother 'cast out by the violence of Cardinal Richelieu', he castigated the latter for having 'no regard for the fact that he is her creature, and that she not only raised him from the dirt but placed him in an eminent position from which he now hurls against her the thunderbolts of his ingratitude'.

60

For the present Rubens was ignored at the French court. The programme had been drawn up by the artist for the second cycle devoted to the life of Henry IV. The surviving sketches show that the active warlike exploits of the king needed no disguising or decorating with allegory. The subject appealed far more than that of the first cycle and Rubens enthusiastically declared that 'the theme is so vast and so magnificent that it would suffice for ten galleries'. By this time he was well enough acquainted with French intrigue to 'believe there will not fail to be difficulties over the subjects . . . which ought to be easy and free from scruples'. His forebodings were to some extent confirmed by the fact that the cardinal had the programme in his hands but refused to discuss it on the excuse that he was fully occupied with affairs of state. With a feeling of despair, Rubens exploded, 'I am tired of this court, and unless they give me prompt satisfaction, comparable to the punctuality I have shown in the service of the queen mother, it may be (this is said in confidence, *entre nous*) that I will not readily return.'

And it was not the only time, and the only court, of which Rubens was to complain.

In retrospect, in his own country, Rubens was calmer but hardly less bitter, 'when I consider the trips I have made to Paris, and the time I have spent there, without any special recompense, I find that the work for the queen mother has been very unprofitable to me'. And he could not help comparing the court of Flanders with the court of France. A relatively small and unimportant court might be dull but it had advantages: 'Here we go on in the ordinary way, and each minister serves as well as he can without overstepping his rank; and in this manner each one grows old and even dies in office, without expecting any extraordinary favour, or fearing disgrace. For our princess shows neither hate nor excessive love, but is benevolent to all.' But as Rubens himself was the first to own, his contacts with the Parisian court were not all a loss. In the first place he made an important new acquaintance in the figure of the Duke of Buckingham, who was to play a large role in the artist's future. On a more intimate level, Rubens made a lifelong friend in Nicolas-Claude Fabri de Peiresc. For posterity it was a particularly rewarding friendship, since actual contact between the two men was limited to a very short period at the beginning of Rubens' visits to Paris, but was later nourished on a correspondence that lasted all their lives.

*Peiresc*     Peiresc, three years younger than Rubens, was a Provençal who had a rugged, uncouth appearance, with sharp eyes indicative of a keen intellect. Ostensibly studying law in Padua, he had become passionately attached to Italian art and history, both ancient and modern, and in his spare time he made himself into a distinguished Renaissance scholar. After his stay in Italy, he had travelled widely in northern Europe, meeting and making friends with scientists, scholars and artists, before he settled in Paris from 1616 to 1623. His meeting with Rubens led to an immediate friendship. Their conversation must quickly have revealed how much they had in common, but their relationship was stimulated by their different approaches. Peiresc was essentially a scholar and antiquarian, who was often as much interested in works of art for the light they threw on the society that produced them, as for their intrinsic beauty. By comparison, Rubens was far more aesthetic in his approach, and considered the work of art itself as the final object of study. But he was no amateur dilettante; 'in matters of antiquity he possesses the most universal and remarkable knowledge I have ever seen' was the considered opinion of his friend. In their letters they discussed detailed and learned points about numerous works of art, and Peiresc was not the only recipient of these discussions. Rubens had been introduced by the Frenchman to the apostolic nuncio in Brussels, and in a long letter to the latter, Rubens 'though deprived of books and my notes' discoursed most eloquently on the Temple of Diana at Ephesus. Allied with his passion for works of art was the phenomenal memory so essential to the scholar, so that twenty years after he had seen the *Aldobrandini Wedding* he was able to give a detailed description of it, adding modestly that 'this is all I can tell you vaguely, *memoriter et ex tempore*'.

Nicolas–Claude Fabri de Peiresc, from an engraving after a painting by Van Dyck

Their mutual interests included collecting. Peiresc had gathered together a large group of antique coins and gems. Shortly after their first meeting Peiresc sealed their friendship with a gift to Rubens, who replied, 'I have never in my life seen anything that gives me more pleasure than the gems you have sent me.' The two of them had already conceived an ambitious project to produce a study of the more important gems, illustrated by engravings made from drawings by Rubens, particularly the Gemma Tiberiana (then in Sainte-Chapelle), which Peiresc had discovered. Peiresc had agents in Asia and Egypt who were busy procuring exotic plants, papyri and so on, indeed, anything which would serve to illustrate the past, so that his house in Provence, which included an observatory, became a museum of entirely heterogeneous objects. He spent the last five years of his life there, cut off from sympathetic friends but protected from loneliness by the vast volume of his correspondence, much of which was used as curling-papers by his niece after his death. It was above all to 'this pearl of honour' in Antwerp that he turned his thoughts; 'I hold there is no more lovable soul in the world than M. Rubin.'

The Gemma Tiberiana,
discovered at Sainte-Chapelle
by Peiresc, and drawn by
Rubens

*Le Chapeau de Paille:*
Susanna Fourment, the
artist's future sister-in-law
(detail) ▶

   Their correspondence did not only cover such learned topics as works of art
and perpetual motion. The times were turbulent, with the balance of power
constantly shifting and war ever threatening, and many of the letters were given
up to relating the latest political events, with which Rubens was particularly well
placed to acquaint his friend, cut off in a small country town. Throughout
Europe there must have been a constant thirst for news which Rubens and Peiresc
did their best to satisfy. When Peiresc left Paris, he introduced Rubens to his
brother, Valavez, who became Rubens' regular Paris correspondent, without
reaching the same intimacy. When it was Valavez' turn to depart from the French
capital, he handed Rubens on to Pierre Dupuy, the royal librarian. To the latter
Rubens wrote lamenting Valavez' departure from Paris. 'I feel the keenest
regret, for I am in truth deprived of the best correspondent in the world. . . . I
should not like to have you assume such a burden but since you are pleased to
honour me with your correspondence it will be enough for you to send me
copies of various public news-sheets of the better sort, but at my expense. . . . I am
sorry we do not have the same convenience here, but we are not accustomed to
news-sheets. Everyone informs himself as best he can, although there is no
dearth of rumour-mongers and charlatans who print reports unworthy of being
read by honest men.'

65

◀ *Henry IV entrusting the*
*regency to Marie de Médicis*
from the Médicis series

At the time when Rubens' name as a painter was becoming known throughout Europe, political affairs were beginning to stir, and in no time he was to find himself caught up in events and forced to become an active diplomat on behalf of his country. In 1621 the Twelve Years' Truce between the United Provinces and Spain came to an end, and the burning question was what was to happen next. Albert and Isabella, with ever-fresh memories of Flanders as a battlefield, wished for nothing more than a continuation of peace. Moreover, their avowed policy was to make Flanders as independent as possible from Spain, and they knew that any renewal of hostilities would result in the intervention of Spanish forces. Philip III, however, had other ideas and was all for subduing the northern Netherlands once and for all, a course of action suiting French policy, which wished for continued hostility between Spain and the United Provinces.

The balance of power was fairly divided. England, France and Spain were the main participants, each at war with one another and anxious to ally the second party against the third. To complicate this infernal triangle, the Emperor of Austria, the Elector Palatinate, the United Provinces and Denmark all provided further treacherous sub-plots with conflicting interests, and the basic enmities of all parties towards one another made complete chaos out of any attempt to discover a pattern in the alignments.

In the struggle between Spain and the United Provinces, Philip III made impossible conditions for resuming the truce. The opening of the Scheldt and therefore the port of Antwerp, which had stood deserted while Amsterdam prospered, was a reasonable request, but when he stipulated that the Dutch should withdraw from the East and West Indies, with whom they had developed a thriving trade, it was obvious that the conditions were intended to provoke an outright refusal. After some abortive negotiations Philip III died in 1621, and was succeeded by his son, Philip IV, without any noticeable change of policy being adopted. Far more serious for Flanders was the death of Archduke Albert a few months later, which, according to the terms on which he and his wife had been appointed regents of the southern Netherlands, meant that the country now returned under the direct yoke of Spain, while the Archduchess Isabella was reduced to the position of governor. A month later Ambrogio Spinola, an Italian general in the service of Spain, marched into the Netherlands as a leader of Spanish forces, and for the next twenty-seven years war was to continue spasmodically until the Treaty of Münster in 1648.

*Diplomatic activity*    Rubens *père et fils* had a way with widows, grass or real, and by 1623 Peter Paul Rubens was in close touch with the Archduchess Isabella on political matters, acting on her behalf as an intermediary between Spinola and the Dutch. Very rapidly he gained her ear with his views as to the conduct of negotiations with the Dutch. Rubens saw himself clearly as the person most suited to direct operations, and with characteristic determination proceeded to take up the role, not without arousing the increasing jealousy and hostility of others, who saw his actions as self-interest against their self-interest. Quite apart from his skill as a diplomat, his

*Surrender at Breda* by
Velazquez

ability to undertake undercover negotiations was greatly enhanced by his profession, which allowed him to travel freely under the guise of pursuing his work as a painter. Throughout the years of his diplomatic activities he succeeded, against all odds, in preventing his painting from becoming a subservient and merely useful pastime. Frequently he was placed in a considerable dilemma, with each activity pulling him in different directions. He was an excellent choice as a negotiator since he was well known in name if not in person at the courts of Europe. The Abbé Scaglia went as far as to say a few years later in tribute to his diplomatic ventures that Rubens was 'a person capable of things much greater than the composition of a design coloured by the brush'. Isabella was desperate for peace, and with his whole heart in such a mission, the artist acted on her behalf. But in spite of extensive activity on the part of Rubens and others, the results were nil, and by 1625 matters were further bedevilled by the death of Prince Maurice of Nassau, commander of the United Provinces' armies, on whose head hopes of peace had been placed, though probably falsely. His successor, Frederick Henry, was faced with a sharp setback shortly after his accession. Breda, a town near the frontier of Flanders, which was strategically placed and, from the point of view of morale, an important position, was forced to surrender to Spinola after nearly a year of siege. The news spread round Europe as a great victory for Spain and was later commemorated by Velazquez' imaginary portrayal of the event. In Flanders

67

The Infanta Isabella
dressed in the habit of
the Order of Poor
Clares, from an
engraving by Pontius
after Rubens (detail)

the boost to morale was celebrated by a visit to the captured city by the governor, who returned to her court by way of Antwerp, where she allowed Rubens to paint her portrait dressed in the habit of the Order of Poor Clares, which she had worn since her husband's death. The painting was engraved and quickly became her official likeness. By this time Rubens, who was firmly in his stride as a diplomat, was the infanta's most trusted counsellor, advising her regularly, either in person or in long letters written while on his various missions. He had a deep admiration for her: 'She is a princess endowed with all the virtues of her sex; and long experience has taught her how to govern these people and remain uninfluenced by the false theories which all newcomers bring from Spain. I think that if her Highness, with the help of the Marquis [Spinola], could govern in her own way, and regulate affairs according to her wishes, everything would turn out very happily.' For his devotion to the infanta, he was repaid by being granted a patent of nobility by her nephew Philip IV. And three years later, in 1627, a more personal honour was conferred by Isabella herself who made him gentleman of the household of Her Most Serene Highness.

68

The Marquis Ambrogio
Spinola by Rubens

The other person who played an important role was the Marquis of Spinola. As an outcome of their frequent discussions, which took place in their joint role as counsellors to the infanta, Rubens had conceived respect and affection for the Marquis, whom he had also portrayed in Antwerp on the occasion of the infanta's visit. After his departure for Spain, Rubens wrote: 'he is the most prudent and sagacious man I have ever known, very cautious in all his plans, not very communicative, but rather through fear of saying too much than through lack of eloquence or spirit. Of his valour I do not speak, since it is known to everyone, and will only say that contrary to my first opinion (I had at first distrusted him, as an Italian and a Genoese) I have always found him firm and sound, and worthy of the most complete confidence.' But the general, like many of his profession, had his limitations, 'for he has no taste for painting and understands no more about it than a street porter'. For Rubens, at this juncture of his political career, this was a surmountable failing, and a few years later, at Spinola's death, he lamented that 'I have lost one of the greatest friends and patrons I had in the world.'

In 1625, when he returned to Paris in order to install the series of paintings devoted to the life of Marie de Médicis, Rubens moved on to a more international stage in his diplomatic career. His visit coincided with the arrival of George Villiers, Duke of Buckingham, who had come to act as escort to Henrietta Maria, whose proxy marriage to Charles I had taken place a fortnight before in the newly decorated Luxembourg Palace. The wedding was celebrated just a year after the abortive and discreditable attempts to arrange a match between Charles and the daughter of Philip III. If a marriage with Spain, intended to help James I's son-in-law, the Count Palatine, to regain his property from the Spaniards, was to come to nothing, then union with France would do equally well. And very shortly afterwards an alliance was concluded between England, France, the United Provinces and Denmark against Spain and the emperor. In all these negotiations Buckingham played an important part, which did not diminish with the death of James I, who had originally been responsible for picking him out as the latest good-looking favourite.

In the course of two years Buckingham had reached a position of absolute power over the king's mind. He was totally unfitted for this role, and both as a statesman and a general proved himself completely corrupt and incompetent.

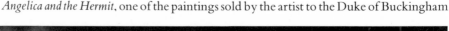

*Angelica and the Hermit*, one of the paintings sold by the artist to the Duke of Buckingham

The Duke of Buckingham,
detail from a drawing
done from life

Rubens was under no illusions about him and only a few months after meeting
him wrote: 'When I consider the caprice and arrogance of Buckingham I pity
the young king, who, through false counsel, is needlessly throwing himself and
his kingdom into such extremity. For anyone can start a war when he wishes,
but he cannot so easily end it.' And only a month later the artist was foretelling
the future: 'as for Buckingham, I am of your opinion that he is heading for the
precipice'. But the duke had his good side, and under the tutelage of his first
patron he had developed a passionate taste for the arts, which never abated,
however low his personal fortunes were. As Balthasar Gerbier, the duke's confidant, put it to Rubens: 'All the machinations of the duke's enemies have never
struck so near his heart as to divert his taste for pictures and other objects of art.'
This common interest gave a special fillip to Rubens' meetings with Buckingham

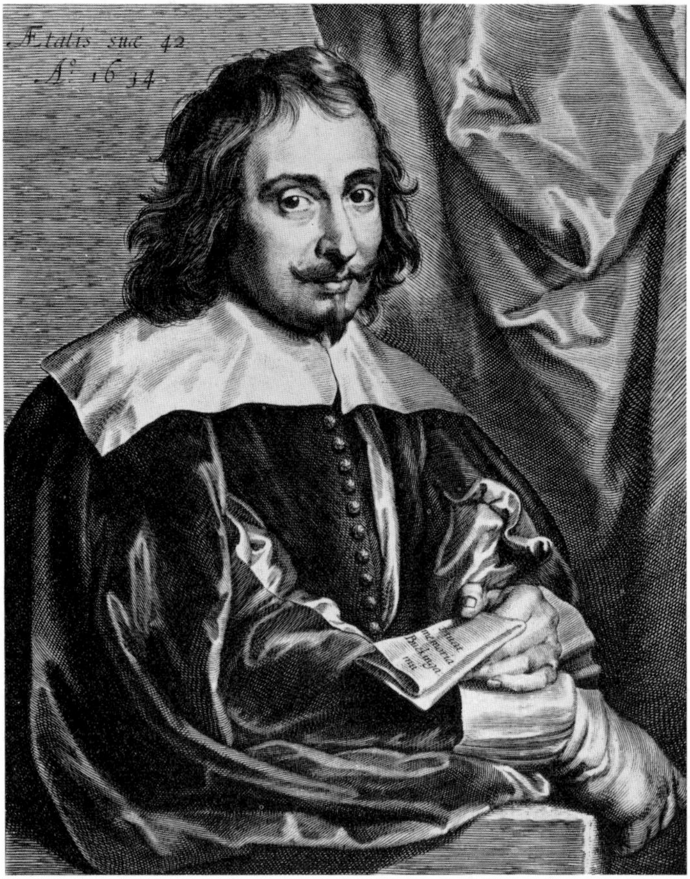

Ætatis suæ 42
A° 1634

Sir Balthasar Gerbier, from an engraving after Van Dyck

in Paris, which later blossomed into a most fruitful relationship between artist and patron. He drew the duke's portrait as well as that of his wife, and painted a large allegorical canvas devoted to the apotheosis of Buckingham for a ceiling in the duke's house. Either before or during their conversations in Paris, Buckingham must have learned of the large collection of antiques possessed by the artist, and negotiations were soon in hand for the Englishman to acquire them. These consisted not only of the antique marbles Rubens had obtained from Sir Dudley Carleton some years before, but also those he had brought back with him from Italy. A price of 100,000 florins was finally agreed upon, to include, in addition, cameos, jewels and, most important of all, thirteen pictures by Rubens. The artist acquired a fortune, a new patron and very considerable prestige.

*Balthasar Gerbier*

At the same time Rubens made the acquaintance of Balthasar Gerbier, with whom he was to have numerous dealings over artistic and diplomatic matters for

Sketch for the *Apotheosis of Buckingham*, painted for the ceiling in the Duke's house at Osterley Park

Design for an oval silver dish with the *Birth of Venus*, made for Charles I

the rest of his life. Gerbier was a shady cosmopolitan, Flemish by birth, with a capacity for inventing indiscriminate and totally fictitious aristocratic connections in all parts of Europe. When he arrived in England he was a small-time portraitist, but on being taken up by Buckingham his fortunes were made. He was employed on various artistic commissions by his master and acted as secret agent as well on numerous negotiations, which brought him constantly into contact with Rubens. After a brief setback, at Buckingham's assassination, he was taken up by Charles I, both as a friend and as an agent for acquiring works of art. He was a man of versatile talents, but thoroughly unscrupulous and disloyal. As artist-diplomat, he was a counterpart of Rubens; while Rubens was known for his integrity, Gerbier was noted for his guile. He always, however, behaved correctly with Rubens, who retained a feeling of friendship for him, no doubt turning a blind eye to his more disgraceful deeds.

74

Though Buckingham may have sung Rubens' praises on his return to the English court, he cannot claim responsibility for introducing his work to Charles I. The mutual admiration of king and painter, which grew with the years, had already started before Rubens left for Paris. Writing to his friend, Valavez, the artist did not hide his enthusiasm; 'the Prince of Wales', as he then was, 'is the greatest amateur of paintings among the princes of the world. He already has something by my hand, and, through the English agent resident in Brussels, has asked me for my portrait with such insistence that I found it impossible to refuse him. Though to me it did not seem fitting to send my portrait to a prince of such rank, he overcame my modesty.' This personal seal to their relationship presents us with an image of the artist in his prime – elegant, dignified, serious, independent, but with all the air of the trustworthy ambassador he was so shortly to become. This self-portrait (see frontispiece) confirms why the artist was so warmly welcomed wherever he went.

The agate vase which for a time was in the possession of the artist and is now known as the 'Rubens Vase'

*The farm at Laeken*

*Death of
Isabella Brant*    In his discussions with Buckingham in Paris, Rubens had attempted to play a
peace-making role by asking the Englishman to try to smooth over with his king
their unhappy visit to Madrid, assuring him that both the Infanta Isabella and
Spinola much regretted the treatment meted out to them by the Spaniards. On his
return to Flanders, Rubens became further involved in detailed negotiations on
behalf of the infanta. The plague had struck Antwerp, and for six months, when
he was not undertaking diplomatic work, he lived on his farm at Laeken outside
Brussels. As he must have pondered the change which was taking place in his life,
weighing personal ambition against his devotion to art, he was struck a grievous
personal blow. In June 1626 Isabella Brant died, probably of the plague. It was
one of those moments which reveal a person's true character, and in a heartfelt
reply to his friend Dupuy's condolences, he wrote: 'You do well to remind me of
the necessity of fate, which does not comply with our passions and which as an
expression of the Supreme Power is not obliged to render us an account of its

76

The artist's sons, Albert and Nicholas,
painted shortly before their mother's death ▶

Isabella Brant. Detail from a drawing made shortly before her death
The artist with Hélène Fourment and child, drawn on the *verso* of the study on the left

actions. It has an absolute domination over all things, and we have only to serve and obey. There is nothing to do, in my opinion, but to make this servitude more honourable and less painful by submitting willingly; but at present such a duty seems neither easy nor even possible. You are very prudent in commending me to Time, and I hope this will do for me what Reason ought to do. For I have no pretensions of ever attaining a stoic equanimity.' Only a very short time before Isabella's death the artist had drawn her with plump dimpled cheeks and kindly sparkling eyes, leaving one in no doubt of the enormity of the artist's loss. It was. however, a stroke of irony that induced him, nearly a decade later, to turn over this moving record and draw a study of his second wife with his eldest child, transforming this sheet into his most personal document.

78

Joachim von Sandrart,
Rubens' cicerone in
Holland

If Rubens had any doubts about the direction which his career was taking, they were quickly resolved after this tragic event, and for the next few years he threw himself wholeheartedly into travelling and diplomatic work. Intense activity was to act as a balm to his feelings. By the end of the year he had been to Calais and Paris, in the vain hope of meeting Gerbier to further negotiations for a proposed armistice between Spain, England and the United Provinces, which had been set on foot by the infanta. The next year, after several further attempts to meet Gerbier, the two painter-diplomats succeeded in coming together in Delft. To the world it was meant to appear that they were discussing the sale of the painter's collection to Buckingham, as well as looking at pictures and visiting artists in various Dutch towns. From the latter point of view, Rubens profited from his visit and was much fêted by Dutch artists, as we learn from Sandrart, who was a pupil in Honthorst's studio in Utrecht at the time. The young German, deputed to accompany the master, described many years later how 'after a banquet organized in his honour by Honthorst he left for Amsterdam, then for

*Renewed*
*diplomatic activity*

79

other towns in Holland, where he spent a fortnight in visiting everything that was remarkable'. Such an innocent explanation for Rubens' visit to Holland did not fail to arouse the acute suspicions of the French and Venetian ambassadors even if they remained ignorant of its actual purpose. But then the English were no less suspicious, and with equally good reason, at the prolonged stay of the Spanish Marques de Leganés in Paris.

The artist's diplomatic role, though accepted by the English, despite Gerbier's complaint that 'Rubens had brought nothing in black and white, and that all he said was only in words', met with strong disapproval in Madrid. In a thoroughly ungracious letter, Philip IV rebuked his aunt: 'I am displeased at your mixing up a painter in affairs of such importance. You can easily understand how gravely it compromises the dignity of my kingdom, for our prestige must necessarily be lessened if we make so mean a person the representative with whom foreign envoys are to discuss affairs of such great importance.' France and England had warmly welcomed 'so mean a person' as diplomatic representative, but Rubens had yet to melt Spanish pride and hauteur. Though the Spanish court held these views firmly on this occasion, these were also used to deflect attention from a piece of political treachery. At the time that Gerbier and Rubens were negotiating on behalf of England and Flanders, Spain and France, unbeknown to both Charles and the Infanta Isabella, had signed a treaty for a joint attack on England. With Leganés' eventual arrival in Brussels from Paris, the news of this secret alliance broke. It was therefore hardly surprising that Rubens' activities were abortive. Still unused to the treacherous behaviour of politicians, Rubens was distressed and dismayed. He was yet to learn, but never to endorse, the double dealing of those who rule.

In spite of this failure, Rubens' interest in politics was now thoroughly engaged, and in his letters to the French royal librarian, Pierre Dupuy, which cover this period of the artist's life, he discourses at length on the course of events. He was clearly in a restless and expectant mood when he wrote to his French correspondent: 'Here we remain inactive, in a state of midway between peace and war, but feeling all the hardships and violence resulting from war, without reaping any of the benefits of peace. Our city is going step by step to ruin, and lives only upon its savings; there remains not the slightest bit of trade to support it.' But he did not have to wait long before he was once again called upon to act as negotiator with Gerbier on behalf of the English crown. The hopeless situation created by the alliance of France and Spain had recently been offset by the disastrous failure of Buckingham's expedition to La Rochelle, which left the English keen to reopen peace talks. On her side, the infanta was no less desirous of peace, as she watched her country suffer more and more from poverty and decay. After a great deal of aggressive intransigence on the part of Olivares, the Spanish prime minister, agreement was finally given for peace negotiations to be opened between England and Spain. Madrid was now disillusioned with the French, who had done nothing to implement their combined assault on England. As Spain hedged

80

Self-portrait (detail), painted 1638–40 ▶

Philip IV, from a drawing done in Madrid

about reopening talks, Rubens increasingly became a centre of attention in diplomatic circles. The ambassador of Savoy, the Danish minister to the United Provinces, and the Earl of Carlisle, acting as ambassador extraordinary for Charles I, were all in contact with the painter. Where others were suspected of deceit, Rubens had the unusual advantage of being trusted. After talking to him, the Earl of Carlisle admitted to Buckingham that 'he made me believe that nothing but good intentions and sincerity have been in his heart'. He had his finger very firmly on the political pulse, and the Spanish court grudgingly acknowledged this by acceding to his proposal that he should be summoned to Madrid to prepare the ground for the discussions.

As usual, Rubens' mission was clouded in secrecy, and as one spectator wrote: 'Rubens has gone to Spain, where he says he is summoned to paint the king.' That the truth was otherwise, suspicious diplomatic observers were not slow to

*Mission to Spain*

◀ The wings of the *Ildefonso Altarpiece*, portraying the Archduke Albert and the Archduchess Isabella

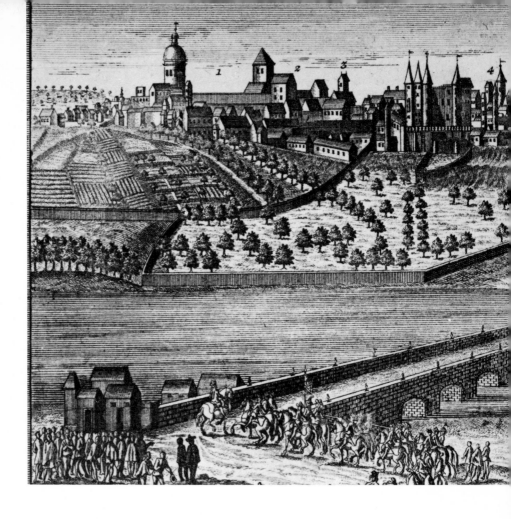

conclude, and in no time all kinds of rumours about his ultimate destination began to circulate around foreign courts. After his arrival in Madrid, observers quickly noted his long discussions with Olivares. The papal nuncio wrote home that Rubens 'often confers in secret with the Count Duke, and in a manner very different from that which his profession permits'. Twenty-five years had passed since his last visit to Spain, and Rubens must have greatly enjoyed the change of circumstances. Instead of being the Duke of Mantua's junior emissary, to be pushed from pillar to post by the duke's jealous agent, he was now a centre of attention and speculation. With pride he must have noted the inquiring looks of senior diplomatic and political figures, who before would have scarcely deigned to give the young painter a glance. It must have seemed to him that his previous rough treatment was atoned for by his present reception. Shortly after Rubens, the two agents of the Duke of Buckingham, Gerbier and Endymion Porter, arrived in Madrid. After lengthy preliminaries, all was set fair for the opening of

82

A view of Madrid from across the river

peace talks, when the news of Buckingham's assassination reached Madrid. Immediately doubts were raised whether England would continue the same policy. Previously Spain had been in a position to play England off against France, but now it was England's turn 'in the middle', and she proceeded to keep Spain guessing for a good six months about her intentions.

After the first hectic weeks of political meetings in Madrid, Rubens' life must have settled down to a waiting calm. Fortunately for him, there was much else to occupy his mind. The country and the people were of great interest to someone as aware of human nature as Rubens. In his comment on the disastrous defeat of the Spanish navy by the Dutch off Cuba, he conveyed something of the bitter and unhappy mood of the country: 'You would be surprised to see that almost all the people here are very glad about it, feeling that this public calamity can be set down as a disgrace to their rulers. So great is the power of hate that they over-look or fail to feel their own ills, for the mere pleasure of vengeance.' More

83

Count Olivares, from the oil sketch by Rubens, with the portrait taken from a painting
by Velazquez

important for Rubens' career were his relations with the king and the prime minister. For the artist it was a triumph of personality. He changed their previous patronizing attitude into one of admiration and trust. This achievement was all the more remarkable, given the very different characters of Philip and Olivares. The latter was austere, stern, quick-tempered and insulting, with a keen disapproval of worldly pleasures. His death wish was strong, and he would frequently lie in a coffin surrounded by monks chanting the *De Profundis*. His energy and ambition for the position of Spain in the world were accepted by the idle hedonistic king, who left his prime minister to run the country. The two men had only one thing in common, a love of the fine arts, and for this Rubens, better than anyone else, was able to provide fuel. But despite all the king's weaknesses, Rubens had a warm feeling for him. He 'alone arouses my sympathy. He is endowed by nature with all the gifts of the body and spirit, for in my daily intercourse with him I have learned to know him thoroughly. And he would surely be capable of governing under any conditions, were it not that he mistrusts himself and defers too much to others. But now he has to pay for his own credulity and others' folly, and feels the hatred that is not meant for him.'

Social intercourse did not, however, occupy all the painter's spare time, and within three months of his arrival in Madrid he wrote to Peiresc: 'Here I keep to painting as I do everywhere, and already I have done the equestrian portrait of His Majesty, to his great pleasure and satisfaction. He really takes an extreme delight in painting, and in my opinion this prince is endowed with excellent qualities. I know him already by personal contact, for since I have rooms in the palace, he comes to see me almost every day.' He reported: 'I have also done the heads of all the Royal Family, accurately and conveniently, in their presence.' In addition to these and other portraits, he made numerous copies of the king's superb collection of paintings by Titian, an artist Rubens had increasingly come to revere.

The arts in Spain were at their prime, with numerous painters and writers such as Lope de Vega and Calderón. But Rubens, wrote Pacheco, 'spent little time with our painters'. Clearly Rubens' unfavourable view of a quarter of a century earlier was little modified, though Pacheco proudly claimed there was one exception, his son-in-law, Velazquez. The two artists had previously corresponded, probably over pictures ordered by Philip from Rubens, but now they had the opportunity to meet and converse frequently, since they both had rooms in the royal palace and were much in the king's favour. The proud father-in-law claimed that 'Rubens praised his [Velazquez'] work very highly because of his modesty.' Unfortunately, we have little other evidence of their contact, and Velazquez' name never once occurs in Rubens' correspondence. Only the portrait of Olivares painted by Velazquez, with an allegorical frame painted by Rubens, done two years earlier, links their names in art. The finished product provides the maximum contrast between the cool, penetrating observation of Velazquez and the rich baroque imagery of Rubens.

*Rubens and Velazquez*

View of the Escorial, painted by Verhulst after a drawing by Rubens

Pacheco also noted that the two artists made a joint visit to that granite treasure-house, the Escorial. Possibly it was on this occasion that Rubens climbed up into the Sierra de Guadarrama and made a drawing of the view, which he recalled so vividly in one of his last letters: 'The mountain, which is called La Sierra de S. Juan en Malagon, is very high and steep and very difficult to climb and descend, so that we had the clouds far below us, while the sky above remained very clear and serene. There is, at the summit, a great wooden cross, which is easily seen from Madrid, and near by a little church dedicated to St John, which could not be represented in the picture, for it was behind our backs; in it lives a hermit who is seen here with a mule. I need scarcely say that below is the superb building of St Lawrence in Escorial, with the village and its avenue of trees, the Fresneda, and its two ponds, and the road to Madrid appearing above, near the horizon. The mountain covered with clouds is called La Sierra Tocada, because it almost always has a kind of veil round its top.'

86

If, like Petrarch on Mont Ventoux, Rubens rushed down to earth again, it was not because of the vanity of the world, but because news had come that England was ready to exchange ambassadors. He was to be sent to London as envoy to negotiate the preliminaries, with the title of Secretary of Philip's Privy Council of the Netherlands, and a personal gift of a diamond ring. He left Madrid, having conquered yet another capital, on his way to another triumph with the third great power. His hoped-for visit to Rome had to be forgone, but by way of consolation he had twenty-four hours in Paris, where he visited Dupuy and other friends, and looked once again at the Luxembourg Palace, where one large room still awaited his attention. Without delay he proceeded to Brussels, where he was immediately received by the infanta and learned the news that perfidious Albion had taken a leaf out of Spain's book and had concluded a treaty with France. His mission to London, therefore, took on an additional urgency, and in a few weeks he had set sail for England in company with his brother-in-law, Hendrik Brant. His life was now so occupied with diplomatic missions that only occasionally could he turn his thoughts to his two sons at home. An affectionate postscript to a letter to his old friend, Jan Gevaerts, shows, however, that his young family was far from being forgotten by its busy father: 'I beg you to take my little Albert, my other self, not into your sanctuary, but into your study. I love this boy, and it is to you, the best of my friends and high priest of the Muses that I commend him, so that you, along with my father-in-law and brother Brant, may care for him, whether I live or die.'

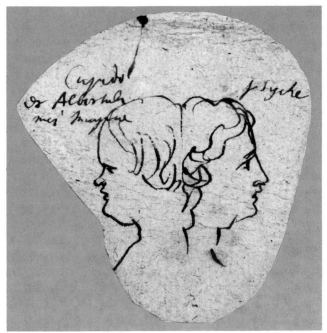

Cupid, in the image of
Albert Rubens,
and Psyche

Greenwich and the Thames seen from Greenwich Park, with Flamsteed House (home

*Mission to
England*

Like many a European, he approached England and its inhabitants with critical thoughts, though it must be admitted that the latest news had given him good cause to complain. 'I am very apprehensive as to the instability of the English temperament. Rarely, in fact, do these people persist in a resolution, but change from hour to hour, and always from bad to worse.' But, like many, he left, nearly a year later, an enthusiastic Anglophile. His admiration for the country was, moreover, entirely reciprocated by its inhabitants. But between his arrival and departure much was to happen, not only to please him but also to try him sorely. All his skill as a negotiator was now put to the test. His previous assignment had been simple compared to the intricate web of different intrigues he met in London, each person acting entirely in his own interests with an unscrupulous disregard for the rights of others. His appointment as envoy had met with approval at the English court, and the chancellor of the exchequer wrote that 'the king is well satisfied, not only because of Rubens' mission, but also because he wishes to know a person of such merit'. The day after his arrival Rubens records that 'the king summoned me to Greenwich, and talked a long time with me,' encouraging the proposed treaty. But before dealing with the conflicting interests of other powers, Rubens noted that England herself presented a maze of different beliefs: 'There are in this Court several factions. The first, which is headed by the Earl of Carlisle, wants peace with Spain and war with France; the second is much larger and wants peace with all. The third is the worst; it wants war with Spain and an offensive league with France against her.' Beyond this, there were the French agents of Richelieu, who were naturally doing all they could to sabotage the progress of the talks. In the struggle for victory no holds were barred, as Rubens quickly realized: 'Public and private interests are sold here for

88

of the Astronomer Royal until 1939) on the left, from an etching by Hollar

ready money. And I know from reliable sources that Cardinal Richelieu is very liberal and most experienced in gaining partisans in this manner.' The Dutch ambassador, who saw in the treaty the end of English aid to his country, was violently hostile. The Venetian ambassador was hardly less so. The future relations with Holland, the Huguenots, and above all with the Palatinate, and through it Austria, were complex by-products of any change in the *status quo* among the three major powers. Such were the vagaries of politics that Rubens found himself in the position of giving financial support, supplied by Catholic Spain, to the Protestant Huguenots in their religious struggle against Catholic France. To add to the complexity of Rubens' situation, he was not empowered to draw up a treaty, as Charles wished and pressed him to do, but only to negotiate a truce. From all sides, his own as well as others, he was hampered by double dealing, inspired by the wish for the other side to play its hand first. Needless to say, such a positive person as Rubens was soon being rebuked for taking direct and constructive steps to achieve his purpose, a course of action that did not appeal to the Spanish taste for evasion and procrastination. Like the other two powers, Spain also wished to weigh up the different advantages of making a treaty with either England or France. The infanta and her painter representative were odd men out in their desire for straight honest dealing.

For three months Rubens negotiated with England for the exchange of ambassadors, regularly sending back detailed reports of events to Olivares. At last his efforts were crowned with success, and agreement was reached. Being an active man, Rubens fondly imagined that his task was at an end, but a further three months passed before the Spanish ambassador's arrival, and several more before Rubens was actually allowed to leave England for home. But in the end

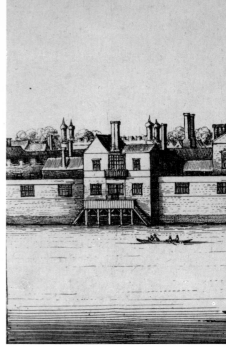

Thomas Howard, Earl of Arundel (detail)

his uprightness paid and he was honoured on all sides. After trying him almost beyond endurance, Spain at last recognized the achievement of her envoy. Reporting to Philip IV about the successful outcome, the Junta gave Rubens 'approbation and thanks for what he had done and written and for the tact with which he had acted in this affair'. A little later Philip urged the infanta to appoint him as her ambassador: 'Rubens is highly regarded at the court of England and very capable of negotiating all sorts of affairs. . . . In such matters one needs a minister of proven intelligence with whom one is satisfied.' And this was written by the man who had not long before described the painter as 'so mean a person'. Helping to encourage this *volte-face* were enthusiastic reports about the painter that were received in Madrid from both Sir Richard Weston, the lord treasurer, and Sir Francis Cottington, the chancellor of the exchequer, who was to be sent to Spain as ambassador and who, before his departure, gave a lavish entertainment in Rubens' honour. Cottington had written that Rubens 'is not only very clever and adroit in negotiating matters, but also knows how to win the esteem of everyone and especially of the king'.

Rubens' mission was largely completed by the end of September, and he had six months to fill in before he was allowed to depart home. He took the opportunity to cast a prolonged glance at the new country around him. And though he lamented that 'to see so many countries and courts in so short a time would

Whitehall from the river, from an etching by Hollar

have been more fitting to me in my youth, than at my present age . . . neverthe-less, I feel consoled and rewarded by the mere pleasure in the fine sights I have seen on my travels.' He had lost none of his intellectual curiosity. Apart from a visit to Cambridge, where he was awarded an M.A., we know little of his actual movements. In London he stayed with his old friend and fellow painter-diplomat, Balthasar Gerbier, in Whitehall. He got to know Cotton the archaeologist, and Drebbel the inventor, and also visited a number of collections of works of art, including those of the king, the celebrated Arundel marbles, and the collection of Buckingham, much of which had come from Rubens, and which still remained in the possession of the duke's widow. He was not slow to note 'that all the leading nobles live on a sumptuous scale and spend money lavishly, so that the majority of them are hopelessly in debt'. His remarks were not inspired by any puritanical spirit, and his warm appreciation shines forth from another letter: 'This island seems to me to be a spectacle worthy of interest of every gentleman, not only for the beauty of the countryside and the charm of the nation; not only for the splendour of the outward culture, which seems to be extreme, as of a people rich and happy in the lap of peace, but also for the incredible quantity of excellent pictures, statues, and ancient inscriptions which are to be found in this court.'

Rubens' most notable personal success was with 'the greatest amateur of *Charles I* painting among the princes of the world'. From the moment Charles met the

*St George and the Dragon* painted by Rubens in London and presented to Charles I.
The Thames valley appears in the background
Charles I and Henrietta Maria in the roles of St George and the Princess (detail left)

artist at Greenwich their relationship flourished, whatever the political climate
might be outside. Like everyone else, the king recognized him as somebody far
above the run of political animals who infested the capital. Rubens must have been
immediately attracted to the glittering life of the court, which numbered such
people as Inigo Jones among its stars, as well as by its keen appreciation of painting.
Though only the Banqueting House had been built, plans were afoot to make
Whitehall one of the largest and most sumptuous royal palaces in Europe. Works
of art worthy of such a setting were already in the king's possession, and it was
fitting that nearly every picture that Rubens had time to paint in England was
destined for one of the finest collections ever to have existed. He made a present
of his *St George and the Dragon* to the king. This was a very personal gift, since
the patron saint bears Charles' features, the princess those of Henrietta Maria,
while the landscape is an accurate record of the blue misty light which is so

93

characteristic of the Thames valley. Finally, on his departure, he gave the king another picture, no less allusive in subject-matter, *Peace and War*, in which his host's wife, Mrs Gerbier, appears as the Goddess of Peace, and her children as those who rush towards her in the composition. In contrast to the court of Spain, the court of St James's encouraged the easy informality of such allusions. The king for his part, as well as laying firm plans for the artist to decorate the ceiling of the Banqueting Hall, knighted Rubens on the eve of his departure, presenting him with the jewelled sword used for the accolade, as well as a ring from his finger and a hat cord ornamented with diamonds. The admiration and affection were entirely mutual. But whereas Charles was most reluctant to let him go, Rubens felt the call of home: 'Although I enjoy every comfort and satisfaction here, and although I am universally honoured, more than my rank deserves, I cannot remain here any longer than the service of His Majesty requires.'

*Retirement from politics*

Rubens had been heavily involved during the last few years in diplomatic missions. So busy was he travelling from one country to another, conducting long and complex negotiations, that the time he had to devote to his art would have made a Sunday painter of a less determined and energetic character. But already in 1629 there were rumours of dissatisfaction with the life he was called to lead. The negotiations in England with all parties procrastinating and changing their minds had wrung a heartfelt cry from the archduchess's ambassador, 'I am longing to return home.' His immediate and ostensible reasons were partly domestic: 'I cannot postpone my departure any longer without great disadvantage to my domestic affairs, which are going to ruin by my long absence of eighteen months, and can be restored to order only by my own presence.' (His brother-in-law Hendrik Brant, who was with him, had, according to Rubens, less serious reasons for his restlessness: 'It distresses him to be so long deprived of the society of the girls of Antwerp. Probably in the meantime they will all have been snatched away from him.') But as future events were to show, Rubens' desire to return home revealed a far more fundamental urge.

One can attribute several motives to Rubens' desire to leave the world of politics. From a personal point of view he had achieved what he set out to do, while at the same time he must have had a gradual feeling of the futility of trying to influence the rulers of the world towards a peaceful and honourable course. At first he can have found it no hardship that his diplomatic activity rapidly increased about the time of Isabella's death. His continued absence from the home where so many happy years had been spent with his wife, and the constant preoccupation with travelling and negotiating, must have provided the necessary distraction. In addition, there was the more permanent driving force of ambition – Rubens himself used the word – which was spurred on by a deep wish to make up for the past. Perhaps his rough treatment as a young man in Spain occasionally came to mind as he ascended the ladder of success. Beyond that there was the memory of his father disgraced, and his mother humiliated. By his own achievements he was atoning for the sadder aspects of the family's past. Finally, the glamour

94

Mrs Balthasar Gerbier
with her children, in
the role of the Goddess
of Peace, a detail from
the painting
*Peace and War*

that went with this way of life was clearly not displeasing to the ambitious artist.

But it would be manifestly unfair to see Rubens' actions in an entirely personal light. His actions were also dictated by more altruistic reasons. He combined a tremendous patriotic fervour, shown in his loyalty to the Infanta Isabella, with a passionate love of peace. The world's fickle interest in peace, which to Rubens came before all else, was a frequent *cri de cœur* in his letters. In every instance his diplomatic role was on the side of peace. The unsettled and threatening atmosphere of Europe, with its inherent dangers for mankind, and above all the fate of his beloved countrymen constantly disturbed him, and the sight of the three great nations playing power politics of brinkmanship was to him a source of incomprehension and distress that people's lives and happiness could be bartered in such a cavalier fashion. But in this field Rubens' diplomatic ventures were

95

ultimately a failure. He was an honest man, struggling in a world where honesty was a handicap, arguing from a position of weakness – his aim was peace and not victory. Today's successes were tomorrow's reversals, and he left the world much as he had found it. He became more and more intolerant of the shifting, vacillating world of court and politicians, where personal vanity and gain were more important than fundamental issues. The art of diplomacy as practised in Europe by the three major countries was the art of saying yes and meaning no, and Rubens' upright character was no match. Even such a distinguished figure as Wotton could describe diplomacy as the art of lying abroad on behalf of one's country. For Rubens, who had left a world of which he was complete master, and in which he had left positive and durable achievements, the quicksands of politics could provide no long-term satisfaction. Increasingly he was overcome by the desire to return to the world where, like the centurion, he could say come, and he comes, and go, and he goes.

This applied not only to those with whom he dealt, but also to his creative urge. Unlike diplomatic manœuvres his pen and brush would lead him to certain tangible results, and as one abortive negotiation succeeded another, his fingers must have itched with the desire to take up his tools and lose himself in his own totally absorbing world. Finally, with a decisiveness and intelligence for the right reasons and the right time, so characteristic of Rubens, he took the right action. 'I made the decision to force myself to cut this golden knot of ambition, in order to recover my liberty. Realizing that a retirement of this sort must be made while one is rising and not falling; that one must leave Fortune while she is still favourable, and not wait until she has turned her back, I seized the occasion of a short, secret journey to throw myself at Her Highness' feet and beg, as the sole reward for so many efforts, exemption from such assignments and permission to serve her in my own home. This favour I obtained with more difficulty than any other she ever granted me.' There were no regrets: 'Now, for three years, by divine grace, I have found peace of mind, having renounced every sort of employment outside of my beloved profession.'

The ivory salt-cellar made by Georg Petel for Rubens from his design, c. 1628

The artist and Hélène Fourment with his son Nicholas, walking in their garden in Antwerp

There was yet another factor besides art and diplomacy in his change of attitude. With superb candour and self-knowledge he explained the recent events in his private life to his old friend Peiresc: 'I made up my mind to marry again, since I was not yet inclined to live the abstinent life of a celibate, thinking that, if we must give the first place to continence we may enjoy licit pleasures with thankfulness.' He explained his choice: 'I have taken a young wife of honest but middle-class family, although everyone tried to persuade me to make a court marriage. But I feared pride, that inherent vice of the nobility, particularly in that sex, and that is why I chose one who would not blush to see me take my brushes in hand. And to tell the truth, it would have been hard for me to exchange the priceless treasure of liberty for the embraces of an old woman.'

98

As in the conduct of his professional life, so in his choice of partner he now knew exactly what was right for him; in this case one must say that his head and heart were perfectly attuned, for this was no cool cerebral decision. By rejecting a middle-aged countess for a very pretty, very young *bourgeoise* he was turning against the milieu in which he had moved for the last five years. With the true self-acceptance that comes in middle age to those with self-knowledge, Rubens prepared to return to the setting in which he had been brought up, and as a result he was rewarded with a glorious Indian summer of peace and enjoyment.

His choice fell on Hélène Fourment, the eleventh child of an Antwerp silk merchant. She was no stranger, since he must have first set eyes on her not later than her fifth year, when one of her brothers married a sister of Isabella Brant,

99

then very much alive. When Rubens and Hélène Fourment married in December 1630 she was no more than sixteen against his fifty-three years, so he would have watched her adolescence with almost avuncular interest. Her role in Rubens' life was quite different from that of Isabella. If one can liken Rubens' first marriage to that of Tamino and Pamina on their journey through fire and water, his second brings to mind the spirit of a very different story, that of Silenus awakened by the water nymph Aegle rubbing his face with mulberries so that he breaks into laughter and song.

From her numerous appearances in his paintings, whether as herself, or as Hagar, or in various slightly different ways as each of the girls in the *Garden of Love*, it is abundantly clear that Rubens was intoxicated by her. Whereas for Isabella he had true love and admiration, he was overcome by infatuation for Hélène. If ever an artist put into practice Renoir's vivid dictum, it was Rubens in his painting of Hélène Fourment, above all in the full-length portrait of her on her way to the bath, wrapped, quite inadequately, in a fur cloak. The tingling vitality and realism of this overpowering presentation of the female nude were quite alien to the Italian tradition. The rejoicing in actual appearance with all its imperfections, according to a classical canon, was far more the taste north of the Alps, and was seen most notably before in the work of Dürer. Whether overcome by admiration or repulsion, the beholder – he is more a voyeur than spectator – cannot remain unmoved. In his own time Rubens was by no means alone in admiring Hélène's opulent charms. Nine years after they were married, the Cardinal-Infante Ferdinand's gift to his brother Philip IV of Rubens' *Judgment of Paris* was accompanied by a letter in which he wrote that 'the Venus in the centre is a very good likeness of his wife, who is certainly the handsomest woman to be seen here'. But if Hélène gratified Rubens' senses and inspired his painting, she did not entirely remain the sweet young thing, even if she was at first swept off her feet by the intensity of passion she had unleashed. Though she was an excellent wife, one suspects more than a touch of an Aristotle-Phyllis relationship which must have given a piquancy to their lives together. One drawing shows her pouting and sulky; her temperament is little hidden in this intimate moment as she sits to her husband.

Upon his marriage Rubens was not to be let off immediately from diplomatic chores. A month afterwards he wrote to a friend: 'I am so disgusted with the court that I do not intend to go for some time to Brussels. . . . My personal ill-treatment annoys me, and the public evils frighten me.' But by the summer of 1631 he was involved once again, this time in the personal cause of Marie de Médicis, who had recently been banished from France by her erstwhile favourite, Cardinal Richelieu, and had fled into the Spanish Netherlands to try to raise an army. Rubens was called in to act as intermediary in the negotiations between the queen mother and Spain, and though he must have accepted with a heavy heart, it was a cause in which he felt deeply. Quite apart from sharing Marie de Médicis' hatred of Richelieu, he was moved by his affection and admiration for her as a

◀ Hélène Fourment wrapped in a fur cloak

queen and a patron; she was yet another widow whose cause Rubens championed. Shortly before this latest event he could say: 'I sometimes think I ought to retire with my family to Paris in the service of the queen mother.' That sacrifice was no longer necessary, and he could take her side nearer home, which he did actively for a year before giving up in disgust. The balance of power made any immediate and effective aid to the queen mother impossible. When help eventually came it was too little and too late, and Richelieu had no difficulty in dispersing the small army raised against him.

After two other small and unsuccessful missions, Rubens' diplomatic career came to a close (apart from one further intervention in 1635), but not before the artist had engaged in a thoroughly unpleasant correspondence with the irascible Duke of Aerschot, the leader of the States-General in Brussels, who considered that Rubens had the archduchess's ear and that he was being by-passed. The petty jealousy of those on his own side caused Rubens as much disgust as the wiles of his adversaries. He wrote to the duke with dignity and respect, yet yielded not one inch. In reply he got the kind of abusive letter which has always been the prerogative of the ill-tempered aristocrat, ending with the words: 'It is of very little importance to me how you proceed, and what account you render of your actions. . . . All I can tell you is that I shall be greatly obliged if you will learn from henceforth how persons of your station should write to men of mine.' Rubens had travelled a long way from his days at the court of Mantua, but the treatment meted out to him was often little better, and this must have amply confirmed him in his decision to return exclusively to painting and his new family.

The Banqueting House, Whitehall, today, built by Inigo Jones and completed in 1619

*The Apotheosis of James I*, the sketch for one of the canvases on the ceiling of the Banqueting House

Owing to the ousting of the queen mother by Richelieu, the projected sequel to the Marie de Médicis series devoted to the life of her husband Henry IV got no further than a number of superb sketches. On the other hand, work on the same scale at the English court came to a glorious conclusion. Grandiose plans prepared by Inigo Jones for rebuilding the palace in Whitehall, after it had burned down in 1619, had advanced as far as the completion of the Banqueting House. As early as 1621, when Rubens was putting the finishing touches to the Jesuit ceiling, feelers were being put out to the artist to see how he would react to a grand scheme of decoration. The idea immediately took fire in Rubens' imagination and he replied self-confidently. Nothing took shape, however, until he returned from his visit to London in 1629, and five years later the large canvases which were to cover the whole ceiling of the hall were ready for dispatch to England. The subject of the nine canvases was the glorious reign of Charles' predecessor, James I; but the events of his reign were in fact no more heroic than those of Marie de Médicis. Once again Rubens had recourse to allegory to bolster up the all too human behaviour of his subject, and it is the allegory of justice and power of the divine right of kings that overwhelms the spectator as

*The Whitehall ceiling*

103

he looks up at the superbly designed ceiling with its lavishly carved rich gilt frame. With more wishful thinking than reality, James I had proclaimed to Parliament that 'The state of monarchy is the supremest thing upon earth. For kings are not only God's lieutenants upon earth and sit upon God's throne, but even by God himself they are called gods.'

A whole year passed before Gerbier was told to accept delivery of the canvases. By this time they had suffered from being rolled up, and Rubens had to retouch them extensively. He was not, however, to be lured from home, 'Inasmuch as I have a horror of courts, I sent my work to England in the hands of someone else.' Two years after finishing the work he wrote to his old friend Peiresc: 'I have not yet received payment, however, and this would surprise me if I were a novice in the ways of the world. But having learned through long experience how slowly princes act in others' interests, and how much easier it is for them to do ill than good, I have not, up to now, had any thoughts or suspicion of unwillingness to grant me satisfaction.' He had learned his lesson, and his resigned cynicism about his royal patrons allowed him to enjoy peace of mind. In the same letter he said 'I have preserved my domestic leisure, and by the grace of God, find myself still at home, very contented.' If King Charles was exceedingly slow in paying for the goods he had ordered (Rubens had to wait another two years for the final payment), he did at least enjoy them, and posterity will forgive the king for his tardiness in settling his debts in view of his genuine admiration. Charles presented the artist with a heavy gold chain and, a sign of real appreciation, gave orders that no masques were to take place there for three years 'by reason the room where formerly they were presented having the ceiling since richly adorned with pieces of painting of great value . . . lest this might suffer by the smoke of many lights'. It was a final irony that on that unhappy day in 1649, the scaffold for the king's execution was erected in front of this very building.

*Last years of the Archduchess Isabella* At the same time as Rubens was trying to escape from his diplomatic work, he was painting the most inspired altarpiece of his career, and possibly of the seventeenth century, for the beloved patron whom he had acted for and advised for over twenty years. It was a glorious end to their friendship. The altarpiece consisted of a central panel depicting St Ildefonso receiving his vestments from the Virgin, and a single wing on each side containing the portraits of Isabella and her husband Albert with their patron saints. The recipients of Isabella's gifts were the members of the Confraternity of St Ildefonso, which had been founded in Lisbon by Albert when he was governor of Portugal, and had moved to Brussels when he became joint ruler of the Netherlands. For Isabella it must have been a happy commission, commemorating her husband and his works by the hand of her trusted adviser and painter. For the occasion Isabella threw off her nun's garb and was seen in her archducal robes some twenty years younger. Rubens gave of his very best and every brushstroke bears the unmistakable touch of the master inspired 'by a violent driving on of the passion', so that the altarpiece has a shimmering unity that marked the supreme achievement of his last works.

104

The central panel of the *Ildefonso Altarpiece,* painted for the Infanta Isabella (see also colour plate, facing p. 81) ▶

A few years later, the Infanta Isabella died. This was just one year after Rubens had thrown himself at her feet and begged 'permission to serve her in my own home'. He was no longer tempted by affection to overcome his unwillingness to get involved in political matters. Plans had been under discussion for some time to decide upon a successor to Isabella who could be familiarized with the ways of the Netherlands. The choice finally fell on Ferdinand, son of Philip III and brother of Philip IV. At first an ecclesiastical career had been chosen for him – at the age of nine he was made an archbishop and two years later he received a cardinal's hat. At the age of twenty, when he took his place for the first time at the Council of State beside his father, he pleaded with him to 'rid me of these cardinal's robes, that I may be able to go to war'. He shared the pleasures of his brother for the arts, hunting and women, but unlike him was to become an active and able ruler. When the infanta died he was not yet ready to assume her place and only a year later did he set out for Flanders from Milan where he had been studying war and politics. On the way he put theory into practice and made a highly successful début as a general in the field when the Swedes were routed at the Battle of Nördlingen.

*Introitus*
*Ferdinandus*
The leading citizens of Antwerp were not slow to invite their new ruler to make a triumphal entry into their city. It was to be a gala occasion and to impress the cardinal-infante, elaborate street decorations were to be erected. The first proposal was fairly simple, but soon the scheme grew to grandiose proportions, and whom better could they choose as chief designer and impresario than their leading painter? Rubens wrote to Peiresc: 'Today I am so overburdened with the preparations for the triumphal entry of the cardinal-infante (which takes place at the end of this month), that I have time neither to live nor to write. I am therefore cheating my art by stealing a few evening hours to write this most inadequate and negligent reply to the courteous and elegant letter of yours. The magistrates of this city have laid upon my shoulders the entire burden of this festival, and I believe you would not be displeased at the invention and variety of subjects, the novelty of designs and the fitness of their application.' In his time Rubens had decorated a whole church, a palace and a banqueting hall, and he was now set to prove that an entire city was well within his compass. Not for mere effect had he claimed 'that no undertaking, however vast in size or diversified in subject, has ever surpassed my courage', and within the space of a few months he showed himself to be the supreme decorator when he presented his plans for triumphal arches and stages throughout the city. The Grand Council felt that such luxury of invention and opulence of decoration ill-suited the present poverty-stricken state of the city, and cut down Rubens' plans to a certain extent. Yet, as the commemorative engravings, no less than Rubens' own drawings and oil sketches, dashed off in the heat of the moment, amply show, it was a display fit for at least a king, and probably no ruler received a more stylish welcome throughout the century. Ferdinand arrived by river, and the next morning entered the city to be greeted by floats alluding to his achievements, his virtues

A sketch for the *Triumph of Ferdinand* (*above*).
(*below*) A sketch for a Triumphal Chariot to
commemorate the victory won by Ferdinand over
the Dutch, 1638

The Cardinal–Infante Ferdinand from one of
the decorations painted by Rubens for his
ceremonial entry into Antwerp, 1635

Fireworks from the
Cathedral tower in
celebration of
Ferdinand's arrival in
Antwerp

and the history of his House. He was saluted by salvoes of artillery and a fanfare of trumpets. From there the procession moved from one decoration to another, welcomed at each point by musicians. For two evenings in succession there were firework displays, the most spectacular of which came from the cathedral tower. Ferdinand stayed eight days visiting and inspecting the decorations and the more permanent sights of the city, including none other than the house of Peter Paul Rubens, and its owner, who lay in bed worn out and ill, unable to take part in the celebrations he had done so much to create. No doubt they ended in the usual Flemish way. As Ferdinand was to describe a few years later after the Kermesse held in the same city: 'After the procession they all went to eat and drink, and to end with they were all drunk, for without that they did not think it a festival here.' And he concluded savagely, 'the people here live like beasts'. All of this is amply confirmed by Rubens in that hectic orgy pulsating with animal vigour which is the subject of the *Kermesse*.

*The Garden of Love* in the Prado, Madrid

Commissions of a more permanent nature poured in during the artist's last years, and he had little time to sit and muse on his past. The spirit of these bucolic years is best caught in that marvellous subject, the *Garden of Love*, which might be considered as a pendant to the more lowly *Kermesse*. It was a hymn to love which was to be echoed one hundred years later by Watteau in his *Departure from the Island of Cythera*. Instead of the never-never-land of the latter's invention, Rubens shows his *conversation à la mode* taking place on a terrace before a richly sculpted pavilion. In the centre a bevy of beauties sit waiting to be plucked like ripe fruit. Around them, those lucky enough to have found an escort, converse, dance or flirt against the sound of water flowing down into the basin of the fountain below from the ample breasts of a woman riding a dolphin. It is hardly surprising that the girls are readily recognizable as variations on the theme of Hélène Fourment, and it is indeed a tribute to Rubens' passion for her that one Hélène should not have been sufficient. Yet the scene that he presented to us is no honeyed fantasy of his own but reflects contemporary customs. A disapproving priest described the habits of the upper classes: 'They used to sit under a green arbour or go on the water to get an appetite, or again in the afternoon they would mount their carriages and make the pilgrimage of Venus, the fashionable walk; when evening came they sang or danced the whole night and made love in a way that cannot be told.' It was Rubens' genius that he did tell it, and we are enchanted.

Kneeling figure, probably a study for the drawing below

One of two preparatory drawings made by Rubens for the woodcuts made by Christoffel Jegher after *The Garden of Love* (detail)

*Works for*
*Philip IV*
During the artist's last years, by far his most important patron was Ferdinand's brother, Philip IV of Spain. There were already twenty-five paintings by Rubens in the king's collection at the time of Ferdinand's arrival in Flanders, and from then on commissions came thick and fast. Philip needed little telling that he had a superb decorator for the asking, and when he built himself a hunting-box just outside Madrid, known as the Torre de la Parada, he did not hesitate to ask Rubens to provide a series of paintings of subjects taken from the *Metamorphoses* to decorate the rooms. The king was in a hurry and, though assisted by pupils and other Antwerp painters, Rubens could not keep up with Philip's impatience. Ferdinand was kept busy trying to urge on the painter, who with characteristic firmness would 'give no precise answer and confines himself to promising that neither himself nor the other painters will lose a minute'. But the royal brothers need not have worried, for a fortnight before this report Rubens had bought

112

*Nereid on a Triton.*
Another sketch for the
decorations in the
Torre de la Parada

himself a copy of Ovid from his old friend Balthasar Moretus, and, to an artist with such a quick and vivid imagination, it required little time to fire his mind with ideas which were then quickly transferred to panel. By the end of the year the whole series, comprising over fifty pictures, as well as roughly the same number for the king's palace of Buen-Retiro, were ready to be dispatched. The oil sketches, which still exist today, testify to the reality which the mythological world held for Rubens. The unfortunate Icarus, all too visibly aware of his fate, really hurtles towards the earth with breathtaking speed, while Triton with a flourish on his conch bears off across the waters his Nereid who weakly gathers up her flowing tresses like leaves, no less aware of her own rather different fate. The world of mythological make-believe suited Philip's tastes and provided a delightful escape from the sombre surroundings in which he lived. It was a place where the senses could reign undisturbed by religious or political matters.

113

*The Judgment of Paris*, with Hélène Fourment as Venus

This series of pictures was no sooner delivered than the Spanish king instructed his brother to commission further works from the artist. It was about this time that Rubens was increasingly troubled by gout, and to another important patron he pleaded that 'the gout very often prevents my wielding either pen or brush, and . . . hinders me especially from making drawings on a small scale'. But the Spaniards allowed him no respite, and among other works he obliged them with another variation on his favourite theme, the *Judgment of Paris* with Hélène Fourment acting as the model for Venus. On this occasion Paris should have been in no dilemma. Certainly the cardinal-infante was not, and he wrote to reassure the impatient king that 'it is without any doubt the best picture Rubens ever painted', though he went on to voice one small criticism: 'The goddesses are too nude; but it was impossible to induce the painter to change it, as he maintained that it was indispensable in bringing out the beauty of the painting.'

By this time Rubens was only an intermittent visitor to Antwerp. He had already announced the change in his life three years earlier: 'To tell the truth I have been living somewhat in retirement for several months, in my country house which is rather far from the city of Antwerp and off the main roads.' The place of his retreat was the Castle of Steen, situated between Malines and Brussels.

*The Castle of Steen*

◄ Hélène Fourment, painted *c.* 1634

115

*The Castle of Steen*

He was no newcomer to country life. A decade before, he had lived on the farm at Laeken. Two years after that he had acquired a country house called the Castle of Ursele to the north of Antwerp. This, however, must have now become too small in view of his large family and his desire to spend an increasing amount of time in the country. A later advertisement for the sixteenth-century property of Steen shows that it was enough to tempt anyone in search of a country retreat: 'A manorial residence, with a large stone house and other fine buildings in the form of a castle, with garden, orchard, fruit trees and drawbridge, and a large hillock with a high square tower standing on the middle, as well as a lake and a farm with farmhouse, granges, various stables and outbuildings, the whole surrounded by moats.' In addition he purchased farmland and woods around the neighbouring villages. With the ownership of a feudal estate, he assumed the title of Lord of Steen, which he held as his favourite honour. It became a garden of paradise which must have been the setting for some of his happiest days.

Unfortunately, though the building and grounds remain, later restorations have largely removed its original atmosphere. To see it as it was in the artist's day we have to turn to the landscapes he painted there, though happiness and pride of possession gave it quite another aspect than that which greets the literal-minded visitor. Instead of the dull featureless stretch of unrelieved flat country, Rubens imagined his house set in open gently rolling country, the lines of the pollard willows and ditches leading the eye into the distant and extensive views, lit by warm beams of sunlight. The ladies of the house take an afternoon stroll around the house, while the life of the country proceeds on its leisurely course around them. The farmer and his wife return from market with their cart laden with a barrel of wine and a calf. The horses, after the hot dusty lanes, must find their progress through the stream a refreshing reminder that home is almost there. Beyond the stream a hunter and his dog, with almost mock solemnity, stalk partridges which, blissfully unaware of their fate, shake their feathers in the evening sunlight. It was enough to banish the cares and exhaustion of one who was tired with his experience of life. It became not just a way of life but a language of art, as for the first time he consistently studied the country in all its variety of light, mood and season. The pulsating vitality which was the driving force of the painter's heroes, sacred and profane, is no less visible in the lush farmland of his landscapes. Above all, it was the evening light that most appealed to his sensibility. The lengthening shadows and the shafts of light from the low-lying sun produced a most nostalgic and elegiac mood in his painting. His imagination did not, however, rest there, and in his artistic daydreams Steen became the setting for medieval tournaments, with knights in armour furiously jousting on open ground beyond the moat. In the background stood the castle, friendly and imposing, waiting to greet the competitors at the end of the day, inviting them to a lordly and lavish banquet presided over by their host. To escape the present-day world of war and diplomacy, Rubens' thoughts took him to an age when chivalry was not dead.

*A tournament before the Castle of Steen*

Even though he lived on a grand scale with a town and a country house, attended by three servants, a valet, a colour grinder, two grooms and three horses, the course of his life was simple and regular. According to his nephew, he went daily to early Mass, before settling down to work, which was accompanied in monastic style by someone reading to him. His library was extensive, but he still continued to purchase books regularly from Balthasar Moretus at the Plantin press. His taste in reading matter suddenly became historical, and histories of the German peoples, imperial Rome, Byzantium, Persia, and so on, were added to his shelves. His social life was severely restricted to a few close friends, and their conversation confined to serious topics. Almost his only recreations were riding and an hour or so spent studying his collection of gems. He had created his own personal world around him, and he wished nothing to break the even tenor of his daily existence. To date he had offered his life up to the outside world, but now the time had come to sacrifice his privacy and rich inner life no longer. He provided his own interests and his own momentum, and anything beyond that orbit was merely a tiresome distraction.

Isabella Hélène, the
artist's and Hélène
Fourment's second
daughter

*His family*    To enjoy it with him Rubens had the companionship of his wife and his
increasing family. In addition to the four children he had by Isabella, Hélène
Fourment gave birth to five: Clara Joanna in 1632, Frans a year later, Isabella
Hélène in 1635, Peter Paul in 1637, and finally Constantina Albertina, who was
born eight months after her father's death. Like his rural surroundings, their
frequent appearance in his work gives us visible evidence of his affection and
happiness. In an unfinished painting executed during the spring or summer of
1636, Hélène Fourment is seated on a stool, with the family dog curled up in
sleep below, lovingly clasping her son Frans, who looks out with the satisfied air
of one who is fully aware of his favoured position as her first-born male. Rather
wistfully, Clara Joanna stands beside them, unable to attract any of the mother's
devoted gaze, while the year-old Isabella Hélène is represented in the panel only
by a pair of outstretched hands. Her eventual appearance in the picture, however,
is known to us from a beautiful chalk study which portrays the plump baby with
hands outstretched and supported on her feet by reins.

120

Hélène Fourment with her children, Frans and Clara Joanna ▶

The proud possessor of such a family did not neglect to leave a magnificent image of himself, though on this occasion the work was not for home consumption but to keep up his status in the outside world. About fifteen years had passed since the lithe, deeply serious face of the Windsor self-portrait, and the experience of the intervening years is clearly revealed in the noble but ageing appearance of his last self-portrait. It reflects the esteem in which he was held by the world around him. Princes and rulers throughout Europe pleaded for paintings. The Cardinal-Infante Ferdinand made him his court painter. Charles I, in addition to previous honours, presented him with a gold chain and a medal worth £300. Their admiration was a pleasing reward, but no longer an essential ingredient of his life. And the poignancy of the careworn face studied in a moment of melancholy introspection is cleverly masked by the panache of the clothes and the knightly gesture of the hand resting on the sword. Painfully reminded by his frequent attacks of gout, he must have been keenly aware that not much longer was left to him to enjoy the pleasures of this world, and before departing he wished to leave for posterity this monumental but utterly human portrait of himself. It is a portrait that leaves the spectator in a mood of reverential awe and admiration for the achievement and wisdom of a great and elderly man.

*Lucas Fayd'herbe*    As if to complement this noble solemn image, fate has decreed that only now, in the autumn of his life, are we able to gain a deeper insight into his personality. In several personal letters to his favourite pupil and assistant, Lucas Fayd'herbe, the warmth of his personality glows through the reserved outer crust like the sun breaking through a protective line of trees in one of his late landscapes. 'My dear and beloved Lucas', he wrote from Steen to the young sculptor who was holding the fort in Antwerp, and he signed himself, 'with all my heart, dear Lucas, your devoted friend', and then he added in a postscript: 'Take good care when you leave that everything is well locked up and that no originals remain upstairs in the studio, or any of the sketches. Also remind William the gardener that he is to send us some Rosile pears as soon as they are ripe, and figs when there are some, or any other delicacy from the garden. Come here as soon as you can, so the house may be closed; for as long as you are there, you cannot close it to the others. I hope that you have taken good care of the gold chain [probably that given to him by Charles I], following my orders, so that, God willing, we shall find it again.' The relationship was more that of father and son than master and pupil, and when the young man was engaged to be married, Rubens wrote him a highly commendatory testimonial as well as sending affectionate wishes: 'I pray also that God will grant you, as well as your beloved, every sort of blessing. I beg you to kiss the hands of your dear one on my behalf and on that of my wife; we shall always be ready at her service and for your advancement'; and then, a few weeks later: 'I have heard with great pleasure that on May Day you planted the may in your beloved's garden; I hope that it will flourish and bring forth fruit in due season. My wife and I, with both my sons, sincerely wish you and your beloved every happiness and complete, long lasting contentment in

Self-portrait, painted during his last years (see colour plate, facing p. 80) ▶

Lucas Fayd'herbe, from an engraved portrait (detail)

marriage. There is no hurry about the little ivory child; you now have other child-work of greater importance on hand. But your visit will always be very welcome to us.' This letter, his very last, was written only three weeks before his death, and its unparalleled warmth and generosity belie the intense pain he was suffering. His own life was ebbing away, and the future, as he recognized, lay with the younger generation.

*Death*    Gout had first attacked him long ago when he was dealing with Buckingham in Paris. In vain he hoped to leave it behind at the French frontier, but two years later was afflicted by it again, this time in Madrid. He was cured by a Sicilian doctor, whose name and address had already appeared on the fly-leaf of the sketch-book van Dyck took with him to Italy. But now 'the visits and torments of this domestic enemy' became increasingly frequent, so that, instead of merely temporarily impairing the use of his hands, it now completely crippled him. The numerous bulletins sent by Ferdinand to Philip IV took on an increasingly pessimistic note. Only a few weeks before Rubens' death Ferdinand announced that he was completely paralysed in his hands and would never be able to wield a paint brush again. Shortly afterwards Balthasar Gerbier gave the same verdict to Charles I. Such was their opinion of Rubens that the royal courts wished to be kept fully informed of his progress. A temporary recovery allowed

The marble of the Virgin by Fayd'herbe, surmounting the altarpiece in the artist's mortuary chapel

him to write or dictate one or two letters, including the one quoted above, though he must have realized that death was near. On 27 May he summoned a notary and made a new will. Four days after he had signed it, Gerbier wrote to William Murray that 'Sir Peter Rubens is deadly sick: the physicians of this town being sent to him try their best skill on him.' And on the same day Gerbier added a postscript to a letter to Charles I: 'Since I finish this letter news is come of Sir Peter Rubens' death.' As he explained in a letter to Inigo Jones a few days later, Rubens' death was caused by 'a defraction which fell on his heart, after some days' indisposition of ague and gout'.

The same evening Rubens' body was laid out in the coffin and placed in the Fourment family vault in his parish church, St Jacques. The funeral service was celebrated three days later 'with sixty tapers, crosses of red satin, and the music of the church of Notre-Dame'. No less than four banquets were held on the day of the funeral. During the next six weeks some eight-hundred Masses were celebrated in Antwerp for the repose of his soul. In the little parish church of Elewijt, near Steen, which he portrayed in one of his most magnificent drawings, they said twenty-four Masses. Due honour was paid to the most illustrious citizen of Antwerp. The painter's coffin was temporarily left in the Fourment family vault, while a more imposing memorial was erected. A few days before his death Rubens had expressed a wish to his wife and children that a mortuary chapel for himself and his descendants, 'if they held him worthy of such a monument', should be built in their parish church. One of his last pictures, the *Madonna and Child with Saints*, was to be placed over the altar, and above that a marble statue of the Virgin carved by his 'dear and beloved Lucas'. In the following year permission was given to build a funeral chapel behind the choir of St Jacques, and not long afterwards the chapel was installed as the dying artist had wished. Guarded by St George and interceded for by no less than two representations of the Virgin, the human remains of Sir Peter Paul Rubens rest there today. The painting, executed in his last style, quietly glows against the stark white setting of the church.

Gerbier announced Rubens' death as laconically as a proclamation of the royal herald. 'Sir Peter Rubens is deceased three days past, so that Jordaens remains the prime painter here.' (Van Dyck rushed back to Flanders to seize the crown, only to follow Rubens to the grave the very next year.) But the direction of Gerbier's thoughts soon became transparently plain. Already in announcing the news of the painter's death to Charles I, he had promptly followed with the comment that 'many fine things will be sold in his auction', and in letters written the same day to William Murray, the Earl of Arundel, and Inigo Jones the main purpose of writing was the same, to alert them to the disposal of Rubens' collection. And, as the sale catalogue makes plain, Gerbier was far from making 'much ado about nothing'; in it, there are listed no less than thirty-seven Italian paintings, thirty-one copies by Rubens after Titian, fifty-three Dutch, Flemish and German pictures, seventeen paintings by Brouwer, ninety-four of his own, as well as a host of others.

Human feelings at the death of a friend and great man were rapidly submerged at the prospect of the disposal of such a collection. Crocodile tears quickly dried at the sight of so much booty. Gerbier was not, however, a lone vulture. The keen-eyed cardinal of France, the man whom Rubens so detested and despised, was not slow on the uptake. His agent plagued Hélène Fourment to allow his master to purchase the *Bath of Diana*, but the widow, in a narrow-minded mood, was reluctant to part with the nudes. On being pressed further, she placed an absurdly high price on the picture, only to have it accepted, and to receive in

*The Madonna and Child with Saints* placed over the
altar of the artist's mortuary chapel in St Jacques, Antwerp ▶

addition a gift of a watch mounted with diamonds from the delighted cardinal.

Rubens' will was detailed and specific. His bequests were not limited to his family, but included people from all stations of life, even down to the gift of a copy after his painting of a *Nymph and Satyr Carrying a Basket of Fruit* to Peter, outrider of the Clarenstraat, for his help in buying a horse. To Hélène Fourment, Rubens left the customary half share, as well as his portrait of her in a fur cloak. She took the opportunity to buy nine others from the estate. To her and all his children, who were specifically granted equal rights, he left all the family portraits of both marriages. To his eldest son, Albert, he left his books and to both him and his brother Nicholas his agates and medals. But when it came to disposing of the vast collection of his own drawings, which contained the wisdom and experience of a lifetime, the true artist in him ordained that they should not be sold until the youngest of his children was eighteen, and only then if none of his sons had become a painter and none of his daughters had married one. But such is the chance of heredity that Rubens, a painter through and through, was unable to produce a glimmering of artistic yearnings among any of his nine children. And so, with the eventual disposal of his drawings, the works of Peter Paul Rubens became hostages to fortune, and we must rest grateful that the wars and destruction of the intervening years have left so much to enjoy.

Terracotta bust of
Rubens by Georg Petel

128

## ACKNOWLEDGEMENTS

The standard biography of the artist still remains M. Rooses, *Rubens* (London 1904) to which, as anyone familiar with that monumental study will quickly realize, I am very deeply indebted. For the artist's letters I have used the translation made by Ruth Magurn for her excellent edition of *The Letters of Peter Paul Rubens* (Cambridge, Mass. 1955), the notes to which contain a wealth of information. For details about the artist's drawings I have relied heavily on J. S. Held, *Rubens, Selected Drawings* (London 1959) and L. Burchard and R.-A. d'Hulst, *Rubens Drawings* (Brussels 1963), as well as the relevant entries in Frits Lugt's catalogue of the Flemish drawings of the seventeenth century in the Louvre (1949). For the rest I have derived information from numerous sources, though I should particularly like to acknowledge most gratefully both the publications and the personal help of Michael Jaffe, Oliver Millar and Justus Muller Hofstede.

129

1561 November. Marriage of Jan Rubens and Maria Pypelinx in Antwerp

1568 October. Parents flee from Antwerp to Cologne where Jan Rubens becomes legal adviser to Anne of Saxony

1571 March. Jan Rubens arrested and imprisoned in the Castle of Dillenburg on a charge of adultery

1573 May. Jan Rubens freed from prison on condition that he lives in Siegen. His family join him and later that year Philip Rubens is born

1577 June. Birth of Peter Paul Rubens in Siegen

1578 May. Pardon granted to Jan Rubens. Family move to Cologne

1587 May. Jan Rubens dies in Cologne. Family move to Antwerp not long afterwards where they live in the Meir

1590 Rubens leaves Rombout Verdonck's school and enters the service of Marguerite de Ligne, widow of Philip, Count of Lalaing

1591 October. Birth of Isabella Brant. Becomes pupil of Tobias Verhaecht, in whose house he lives

1592(?) Enters studio of Adam van Noort

1596(?) Enters studio of Otto van Veen

1598 Becomes Master of the Guild of St Luke, Antwerp

1599 Triumphal Entry of Archduke Albert and Archduchess Isabella into Antwerp. Decorations prepared in the studio of Otto van Veen March. Birth of Anthony van Dyck

1600 May. Departs for Italy arriving in Venice by July. Meets Vincenzo de Gonzaga, Duke of Mantua, and enters his service
October. Attends proxy marriage of Marie de Médicis and Henry IV in Florence

1601 August. First visit to Rome
October. Maria Pypelinx sells house in the Meir and moves to the Kloosterstraat

1602 April. Returns to Mantua
June/July. Meets his brother, Philip, and Jan Woverius in Verona

1603 March. Leaves for Spain, taking gifts from Gonzaga to Philip III and the Duke of Lerma

1604 Returns to Mantua early in the year

1605 November/December. Second visit to Rome. Stays with Philip in Strada della Croce near the Piazza di Spagna

1606 Begins altarpiece for the Chiesa Nuova

1607 July/August. Stay in Rome interrupted by visit to Genoa in the retinue of Vincenzo de Gonzaga

1608 October. Leaves Rome hastily for Antwerp, only to find on his arrival that his mother has already died. Lives with his brother Philip in the family house in the Kloosterstraat

1609 April. Twelve Years' Truce signed
September. Appointed court painter to Albert and Isabella
October. Marries Isabella Brant at the Abbey of St Michael, Antwerp, and goes to live in his father-in-law's house in St Michielsstraat

1610 June. Commissioned to paint the altarpiece of the *Raising of the Cross* for the church of St Walburga
November. Purchased property on the Wapper where he built his house and studio

1611 March. Baptism of their first child Clara Serena
September. Commissioned by Guild of Arquebusiers to paint altarpiece of the *Descent from the Cross* for the Church of Notre-Dame. The central panel was completed in 1612 and the two shutters two years later

1614 April. Birth of Hélène Fourment (Rubens' second wife)
June. Birth of their elder son Albert

1616 From the beginning of the year they lived in their new house on the Wapper which was finally completed the following year

1618 March. Birth of their younger son Nicholas
April. Concludes agreement with Sir Dudley Carleton to exchange twelve paintings for Carleton's collection of marbles

1619 First exchange of letters with Nicolas-Claude Fabri de Peiresc

1620 March. Commissioned by Jesuits to paint, with the assistance of van Dyck, thirty-nine paintings for the ceilings of the aisles and gallery in their new church in Antwerp

1621 March. Death of Philip III of Spain. Accession of his son, Philip IV
April. End of Twelve Years' Truce
July. Death of Archduke Albert in Brussels

1622 January/February. Visits Paris and signs contract with Marie de Médicis to decorate two galleries in the new Luxembourg Palace. Meets Peiresc

1623 May/June. Second visit to Paris,

bringing nine of the first series of paintings with him
By September. Enters politics
After October. Death of Clara Serena Rubens

1624 June. Philip IV grants Rubens a patent of nobility
August. Peiresc leaves Paris for Provence and his brother, Palamède de Fabri, Sieur de Valavez, becomes Rubens' correspondent in the French capital

1625 February. Arrives in Paris with the outstanding paintings for the Marie de Médicis series
April. Death of James I and accession of Charles I
Death of Prince Maurice of Nassau
May. Attends in Paris proxy marriage of Charles I and Henrietta Maria, daughter of Marie de Médicis. Shortly afterwards Rubens meets the Duke of Buckingham and paints his portrait
June. Fall of Breda to the Spanish troops under Ambrogio Spinola
Arrives in Antwerp from Paris
July. The Infanta Isabella visits Rubens' house on her return from Breda. He paints her portrait dressed in the Order of Poor Clares
August. Until February of the following year lives at Laeken, near Brussels in order to avoid the plague
September/October. Summoned to Dunkirk by the Infanta and sent on a secret mission to the German frontier
November. Duke of Buckingham visits Rubens' house on his way to The Hague in order to conclude treaty between England and Holland

1626 March. Peace Treaty signed between France and Spain
April. Pierre Dupuy, the royal librarian, takes over Valavez' place as Rubens' Paris correspondent
June. Death of Isabella Brant in Antwerp

December. Goes to Calais to ship works of art he had sold to the Duke of Buckingham. He fails to meet the duke's agent Balthasar Gerbier at Calais in connexion with negotiations for a proposed armistice between Spain, England and the United Provinces. Rubens then goes to Paris

1627 Granted title of gentleman of the household of Her Most Serene Highness by the Infanta Isabella
July. Visits Breda, and then to Holland. Meets Gerbier in Delft and together they visit Amsterdam and Utrecht
October. Makes second short visit to Holland

1628 May. The Earl of Carlisle meets Rubens in Antwerp
August. Rubens departs for Madrid, visiting La Rochelle *en route*
September. The assassination of the Duke of Buckingham
October. Capture of La Rochelle

1629 April. Peace between France and England
Leaves Madrid for Brussels, spending twenty-four hours in Paris
June. Embarks at Dunkirk for London; the day after his arrival he is received by Charles I at Greenwich
October. Made Master of Arts at Cambridge
November. Sir Francis Cottington departs for Madrid as ambassador

1630 January. The Spanish ambassador, Don Carlos Coloma, arrives in London
March. Final audience with Charles I, who knights him and presents him with gifts. Leaves for Antwerp the following day
June. Treaty signed between France and Holland
December. Marries Hélène Fourment
Proclamation of peace between England and Spain

1631 February. Marie de Médicis quarrels with her son Louis XIII and is exiled by Cardinal Richelieu. In September she visits Antwerp where she meets Rubens who acts on her behalf
July. Knighted by Philip IV
December. Sent by the Infanta on a secret mission to Frederick Henry in The Hague

1632 January. Birth of Clara Joanna, his first child by Hélène Fourment
August. Visits to Liège and Maastricht to negotiate peace with the States General of the United Provinces
Blessing of altar of the Confraternity of St Ildefonso in Brussels

1633 January. Having asked for passport to The Hague, meets with very strong opposition from the States General in Brussels. Exchange of letters with the Duke of Aerschot
July. Birth of Frans Rubens
December. Death of the Infanta Isabella in Brussels

1634 April. Treaty between France and Holland to continue the war
By August. Completes paintings commissioned by Charles I to decorate the ceiling of the Banqueting House, Whitehall

November. The Cardinal-Infante Ferdinand enters Brussels

1635 April. Triumphal Entry of Ferdinand into Antwerp
May. Birth of Isabella Hélène
Purchases Lordship of Steen, near Elewijt
August. Finally abandons all connections with politics

1636 Commissioned by Philip IV to decorate his hunting-box, the Torre de la Parada, near Madrid
April. Appointed court painter to Ferdinand

1637 March. Birth of Peter Paul
June. Death of Peiresc

1640 May. Dies in Antwerp. Funeral service in the Church of St Jacques three days later

1641 February. Birth of Constantina Albertina

1642 March/June. Auctions of Rubens' collections in Antwerp

1643 November. Mortuary chapel completed and Rubens interred there

1657 August. Auction of Rubens' collection of his own drawings

# NOTES ON THE PICTURES

*Page numbers with an asterisk refer to a colour plate on the facing page. Measurements, given in centimetres, are for the whole picture, not details. Height precedes width*

*Frontispiece.* SELF PORTRAIT by Rubens
  *c.* 1624. H.M. the Queen, Windsor Castle
  Panel. 86 × 62·5
  *Reproduced by gracious permission of Her Majesty Queen Elizabeth II*

*Page*

5 ANTWERP FROM THE RIVER
  (detail). British Museum, London
  Engraving. 8 × 25

6 ANTWERP TOWN HALL IN FLAMES.
  Detail of a painting by an Antwerp Master of the sixteenth century
  Musée Royal des Beaux-Arts, Antwerp
  *Photo ACL*

7 THE CASTLE OF DILLENBURG by Frans Post
  1645. British Museum, London
  Chalk and wash
  *Photo British Museum*

8 SIEGEN
  Sixteenth century. British Museum, London
  Engraving. 10 × 14·5

9 SHEET OF STUDIES INCLUDING SILENUS SURPRISED BY AEGLE by Rubens
  *c.* 1612. H.M. the Queen, Windsor Castle
  Pen and wash. 28 × 50·7
  *Reproduced by gracious permission of Her Majesty Queen Elizabeth II*

11 COPIES AFTER TOBIAS STIMMER by Rubens. Above, Balaam and his ass; below, the ass of the disobedient prophet
  Before 1600. Louvre, Paris
  Pen. 17·2 × 8·2

135

SHEET OF STUDIES FROM THE COSTUME
BOOK by Rubens
Before 1600. British Museum,
London
Pen and wash. 30·6 × 20·7

12 ADAM VAN NOORT by Van Dyck
*c.* 1632 or 1634–5. British Museum,
London
Etching. 15·8 × 24·8

13 COPY AFTER TITIAN'S 'ABRAHAM AND
ISAAC' by Rubens
*c.* 1600. Albertina, Vienna
Chalk and pen. 33·2 × 24·8
*Photo Albertina, Vienna*

14 MANTUA
British Museum, London
Engraving. 10 × 14·5

15 CAMERA DEGLI SPOSI, PALAZZO DUCALE,
Mantua, with frescoes by Mantegna
1474
*Photo Mansell-Alinari*

GARDEN FRONT, PALAZZO DEL TE,
Mantua, designed by Giulio Romano
1525–6
*Photo Georgina Masson*

16 COPY AFTER LEONARDO'S 'BATTLE OF
ANGHIARI' by Rubens
*c.* 1600. Louvre, Paris
Chalk, pen and brush. 45·2 × 63·7
*Photo Giraudon*

17 COPY AFTER MICHELANGELO'S 'CREA-
TION OF EVE' by Rubens
1601–8. Louvre, Paris
Chalk and oil. 26 × 31
*Photo Giraudon*

18 CHRIST CROWNED WITH THORNS by
Rubens
1602. Herzog Anton Ulrich-
Museum, Brunswick
Pen. 20·7 × 28·8
*Photo Herzog Anton Ulrich-Museum,
Brunswick*

19 JUSTUS LIPSIUS AND HIS FRIENDS by
Rubens

*c.* 1612. Pitti Palace, Florence
Panel. 167 × 143
*Photo Mansell-Alinari*

20 PHILIP III ON HORSEBACK by Velazquez
1628. Prado, Madrid
Canvas. 300 × 314
*Photo Mas*

21 VALLADOLID
British Museum, London
Engraving. 18 × 24

22 A RIDER ON HORSEBACK by Rubens
(study for the portrait of the Duke of
Lerma)
1603. Louvre, Paris
Chalk and pen. 30 × 21·8
*Photo Giraudon*

23 LANDSCAPE NEAR MADRID by Bolswert
after a painting (*c.* 1628) by Rubens
in the Johnson Coll., Philadelphia
British Museum, London
Engraving. 33 × 45

24 THE GONZAGA FAMILY ADORING THE
TRINITY (fragment) by Rubens
1604–5. Palazzo Ducale, Mantua
Canvas. 190 × 250
*Photo Mansell-Alinari*

25 THE RUINS ON THE PALATINE by
Bolswert after a painting (*c.* 1610) by
Rubens in the Louvre, Paris
British Museum, London
Engraving. 32 × 45

26 ILLUSTRATION FROM PHILIP RUBENS,
'ELECTORUM LIBRI II', Antwerp, 1608,
vol. II, opp. p. 33. Engraving after a
design by Rubens
British Museum, London

27 PHILIP RUBENS by Cornelis Galle after
Rubens
British Museum, London
Engraving. 20·9 × 13·3

28 ILLUSTRATION FROM RUBENS, 'PALLAZZI
DI GENOVA', Antwerp, 1622, vol. II,
pl. 30
British Museum, London

29 THE MADONNA ADORED BY SAINTS by Rubens
1608. Museum, Grenoble
Canvas. 474 × 286
*Photo Studio Piccardy*

THE MADONNA ADORED BY ANGELS by Rubens
1608. Akademie der Bildenden Künste, Vienna
Canvas. 86 × 57
*Photo Akademie der Bildenden Künste, Vienna*

31 TOWN HALL AND MARKET PLACE, Antwerp
1648. British Museum, London
Engraving. 22 × 34

33 ARCHDUKE ALBERT by Rubens
*c.* 1609. Kunsthistorisches Museum, Vienna
Panel. 105 × 74
*Photo Kunsthistorisches Museum, Vienna*

INFANTA ISABELLA CLARA EUGENIA by Rubens
*c.* 1609. Kunsthistorisches Museum, Vienna
*Photo Kunsthistorisches Museum, Vienna*

34 JAN BRANT by Rubens
1635. Alte Pinakothek, Munich
Panel. 110 × 95
*Photo Bayer. Staatsgemäldesamm-lungen, Munich*

35 THE ARTIST AND ISABELLA BRANT by Rubens
1609. Alte Pinakothek, Munich
Canvas. 178 × 136
*Photo Bayer. Staatsgemäldesamm-lungen, Munich*

36 BIRD'S EYE VIEW OF ANTWERP (from *Introitus Ferdinandi, 1635*, Antwerp, 1642)
British Museum, London
Engraving

37 THE COURTYARD OF RUBENS' HOUSE, Antwerp, by Harrewijn 1684
British Museum, London
Engraving. 28·7 × 35·7

THE GARDEN OF RUBENS' HOUSE, Antwerp by Harrewijn 1692
British Museum, London
Engraving. 33 × 43·4

38 THE INTERIOR OF THE HOUSE OF AN ART COLLECTOR by a Flemish seventeenth-century artist
Nationalgalerie, Stockholm

39 THE COUNTESS OF ARUNDEL WITH SIR DUDLEY CARLETON, AND HER DWARF ROBIN by Rubens
1620. Alte Pinakothek, Munich
Canvas, 261 × 265
*Photo Bayer. Staatsgemäldesamm-lungen, Munich*

40 A LION by Rubens
*c.* 1616. British Museum, London
Chalk and wash. 28·3 × 42·9

41 NICOLAAS ROCKOX by Rubens
*c.* 1614. Musée Royal des Beaux-Arts, Antwerp
Panel. 146 × 55

ADRIENNE ROCKOX by Rubens
*c.* 1614. Musée Royal des Beaux-Arts, Antwerp
Panel. 146 × 55

42 THE INTERIOR OF ROCKOX'S HOUSE by Frans Francken the Younger
Schloss Schleissheim, Munich
*Photo Bayer. Staatsgemäldesamm-lungen, Munich*

43 SAMSON AND DELILAH by Rubens
*c.* 1610. Van Regteren Altena Coll., Amsterdam
Pen and brush. 16·4 × 16·2

44 DESCENT FROM THE CROSS by Rubens (central panel)
1612. The Cathedral, Antwerp
Panel. 420 × 310
*Photo ACL*

137

*Notes*    45  PLANTIN'S PRINTER'S MARK by Rubens
                *c.* 1635. Musée Plantin Moretus,
                Antwerp
                Pen and wash, 20·6 × 27·7
                *Photo ACL*

                JUSTUS LIPSIUS by Rubens
                1615. British Museum, London
                Pen. 23·2 × 18·5

         46  SELF PORTRAIT by Van Dyck
                *c.* 1614. Akademie der Bildenden
                Künste, Vienna
                Panel. 43 × 32·5
                *Photo Akademie der Bildenden Künste,
                Vienna*

         48  LUCAS VORSTERMAN by Van Dyck
                1631. Fitzwilliam Museum, Cam-
                bridge
                Chalk. 24·3 × 17·6
                *Photo Stearn and Sons*

         49  SELF PORTRAIT by Rubens
                *c.* 1614. Uffizi, Florence
                *Photo Mansell–Alinari*

         50  LETTER FROM RUBENS TO SIR DUDLEY
                CARLETON dated May 26, 1618,
                Antwerp
                Public Record Office, London
                *Photo Public Record Office, London*

         52  INTERIOR OF THE JESUIT CHURCH,
                ANTWERP by Sebastian Vrancx
                Kunsthistorisches Museum, Vienna
                Panel. 52 × 71
                *Photo Kunsthistorisches Museum,
                Vienna*

         53  ST CECILIA by Rubens
                1620. Akademie der Bildenden
                Künste, Vienna
                Panel. 27·7 × 42·7
                *Photo Akademie der Bildenden
                Künste, Vienna*

         54  AN ANGEL BLOWING A TRUMPET by
                Rubens
                *c.* 1620. Pierpont Morgan Library,
                New York
                Chalk. 24·5 × 28·3

                *Photo Pierpont Morgan Library, New
                York*

         55  THE LUXEMBOURG PALACE by Israel
                Sylvestre
                Etching
                *Photo Courtauld Institute of Art,
                University of London*

         56  THE PONT-NEUF, PARIS by Jacques
                Callot
                *c.* 1630. British Museum, London
                Etching. 16 × 33·5

         57  MARIE DE MÉDICIS by Rubens
                *c.* 1622. Victoria and Albert Museum,
                London
                Chalk. 34 × 24·7
                *Photo Victoria and Albert Museum,
                Crown Copyright*

         58  THE MARRIAGE OF MARIE DE MÉDICIS
                by Rubens
                *c.* 1625. Louvre, Paris
                Canvas. 394 × 295
                *Photo Giraudon*

         59  MARIE DE MÉDICIS LANDING AT
                MARSEILLES by Rubens
                *c.* 1625. Louvre, Paris
                Canvas. 394 × 295
                *Photo Giraudon*

         60  CARDINAL RICHELIEU by Philippe de
                Champaigne
                National Gallery, London
                Canvas. 58 × 72
                *Photo National Gallery, London*

         61  THE MARRIAGE OF MARIE DE MÉDICIS
                AND HENRY IV by Rubens
                *c.* 1628. Wallace Collection, London
                Panel. 23 × 12
                *Reproduced by permission of the Trustees
                of the Wallace Collection, Crown
                Copyright*

         63  NICOLAS–CLAUDE FABRI DE PEIRESC
                after a painting by Van Dyck
                British Museum, London
                Engraving

138

1630–2. Kunsthistorisches Museum,
Vienna
Central panel. 352 × 236
*Photo Kunsthistorisches Museum,*
*Vienna*

107 THE TRIUMPH OF FERDINAND by
Rubens
1635. Hermitage, Leningrad
Canvas. 150 × 73
*Photo SCR Photo Library*

A TRIUMPHAL CHARIOT by Rubens
1638. Musée Royal des Beaux Arts,
Antwerp
Panel. 103 × 71
*Photo ACL*

THE CARDINAL–INFANTE FERDINAND
by Rubens
1635. Kunsthistorisches Museum,
Vienna
Canvas. 260 × 112
*Photo Kunsthistorisches Museum,*
*Vienna*

108 FIREWORKS FROM ANTWERP CATHEDRAL
engraved by Theodor van Thulden
for *Introitus Ferdinandi, 1635,*
Antwerp, 1642
British Museum, London
Engraving

109 STUDIES OF DANCING COUPLES by
Rubens
*c.* 1636. British Museum, London
Pen. 58·2 × 50·2

110 THE GARDEN OF LOVE by Rubens
*c.* 1635. Prado, Madrid
Canvas. 198 × 283
*Photo Mas*

111 A YOUNG WOMAN KNEELING by Rubens
*c.* 1632–3. Louvre, Paris
Chalk. 40·3 × 47·2
*Photo Giraudon*

THE GARDEN OF LOVE (left half) by
Rubens
*c.* 1632–3. Metropolitan Museum,
New York
Chalk, pen and brush. 48 × 71

112 THE FALL OF ICARUS by Rubens    *Notes*
1636. Musées Royaux des Beaux-
Arts, Brussels
Panel. 27 × 27
*Photo ACL*

113 NEREID ON A TRITON by Rubens
1636. Museum Boymans van
Beuningen, Rotterdam
Panel. 14 × 14
*Photo Museum Boymans van Beuningen,*
*Rotterdam*

114 HÉLÈNE FOURMENT by Rubens
*c.* 1631. Alte Pinakothek, Munich
Panel. 97 × 68
*Photo Bayer. Staatsgemäldesamm-*
*lungen, Munich*

115 THE JUDGMENT OF PARIS by Rubens
1639. Prado, Madrid
Canvas. 199 × 379
*Photo Mas*

116–7 THE CASTLE OF STEEN by Rubens
1636. National Gallery, London
Panel. 134 × 236
*Photo National Gallery, London*

119 A TOURNAMENT BEFORE THE CASTLE OF
STEEN by Rubens
1635–40. Louvre, Paris
Panel. 73 × 108
*Photo Giraudon*

120 ISABELLA HÉLÈNE RUBENS by Rubens
*c.* 1636. Louvre, Paris
Chalk. 39·8 × 28·7
*Photo Giraudon*

121 HÉLÈNE FOURMENT WITH HER CHILDREN
by Rubens
*c.* 1636. Louvre, Paris
Panel. 113 × 82
*Photo Giraudon*

123 SELF PORTRAIT by Rubens
1638–40. Kunsthistorisches Museum,
Vienna
Canvas. 109·5 × 85
*Photo Kunsthistorisches Museum,*
*Vienna*

*Notes*

124 LUCAS FAYD'HERBE after a painting by
G. Coques
*c.* 1661. British Museum, London
Engraving. 19 × 13

125 THE VIRGIN by Fayd'herbe
St Jacques, Antwerp
Marble
*Photo ACL*

127 THE MADONNA AND CHILD WITH
SAINTS by Rubens
1635–40. St Jacques, Antwerp
Panel. 211 × 195
*Photo ACL*

128 PETER PAUL RUBENS by Georg Petel
1633. Musée Royal des Beaux Arts,
Antwerp
Terracotta. Ht. 68
*Photo ACL*

# INDEX

*Numbers in italics refer to illustrations.*
*Asterisks indicate colour plates*